THE
LENAPES

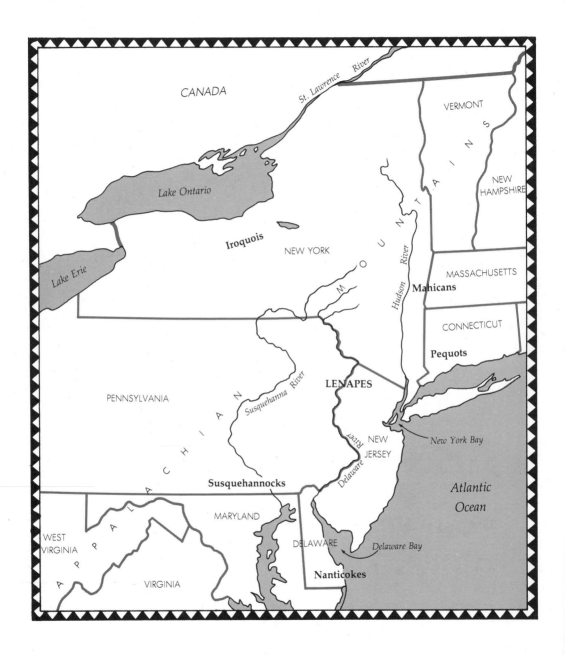

THE
LENAPES

Robert S. Grumet

National Park Service

Frank W. Porter III
General Editor

CHELSEA HOUSE PUBLISHERS
New York   Philadelphia

#1945592

On the cover   A late-19th-century Delaware pouch decorated with beadwork in a floral pattern

Chelsea House Publishers
Editor-in-Chief   Nancy Toff
Executive Editor   Remmel T. Nunn
Managing Editor   Karyn Gullen Brown
Copy Chief   Juliann Barbato
Picture Editor   Adrian G. Allen
Art Director   Maria Epes
Manufacturing Manager   Gerald Levine

Indians of North America
Senior Editor   Liz Sonneborn

Staff for **THE LENAPES**
Associate Editor   Clifford Crouch
Deputy Copy Chief   Nicole Bowen
Copy Editor   Lisa S. Fenev
Editorial Assistant   Claire Wilson
Assistant Art Director   Loraine Machlin
Designer   Donna Sinisgalli
Designer Assistant   James Baker
Picture Researcher   Brian Lindstrom
Production Coordinator   Joseph Romano

3   5   7   9   8   6   4

Library of Congress Cataloging-in-Publication Data

Grumet, Robert Steven.
The Lenapes / Robert S. Grumet : Frank W. Porter III, general editor.
    p.   cm.—(Indians of North America)
Bibliography: p.
Includes index.
Summary: Examines the history, culture, and changing fortunes of the Lenape (also known as Delaware) Indians.
ISBN 1-55546-712-1.
    0-7910-0385-X (pbk.)
1. Delaware Indians—Juvenile literature. 2. Indians of North America—Delaware—Juvenile literature. [1. Delaware Indians.   2. Indians of North America.] I. Porter, Frank W., 1947 –. II. Title. III. Series: Indians of North America (Chelsea House Publishers)   89-940
E99.D2G78   1989   CIP
975.1'00497—dc19   AC

CONTENTS

INDIANS OF NORTH AMERICA

CHELSEA HOUSE PUBLISHERS

INDIANS OF NORTH AMERICA: CONFLICT AND SURVIVAL

Frank W. Porter III

The Indians survived our open intention of wiping them out, and since the tide turned they have even weathered our good intentions toward them, which can be much more deadly.

John Steinbeck
America and Americans

When Europeans first reached the North American continent, they found hundreds of tribes occupying a vast and rich country. The newcomers quickly recognized the wealth of natural resources. They were not, however, so quick or willing to recognize the spiritual, cultural, and intellectual riches of the people they called Indians.

The Indians of North America examines the problems that develop when people with different cultures come together. For American Indians, the consequences of their interaction with non-Indian people have been both productive and tragic. The Europeans believed they had "discovered" a "New World," but their religious bigotry, cultural bias, and materialistic world view kept them from appreciating and understanding the people who lived in it. All too often they attempted to change the way of life of the indigenous people. The Spanish conquistadores wanted the Indians as a source of labor. The Christian missionaries, many of whom were English, viewed them as potential converts. French traders and trappers used the Indians as a means to obtain pelts. As Francis Parkman, the 19th-century historian, stated, "Spanish civilization crushed the Indian; English civilization scorned and neglected him; French civilization embraced and cherished him."

7

Nearly 500 years later, many people think of American Indians as curious vestiges of a distant past, waging a futile war to survive in a Space Age society. Even today, our understanding of the history and culture of American Indians is too often derived from unsympathetic, culturally biased, and inaccurate reports. The American Indian, described and portrayed in thousands of movies, television programs, books, articles, and government studies, has either been raised to the status of the "noble savage" or disparaged as the "wild Indian" who resisted the westward expansion of the American frontier.

Where in this popular view are the real Indians, the human beings and communities whose ancestors can be traced back to ice-age hunters? Where are the creative and indomitable people whose sophisticated technologies used the natural resources to ensure their survival, whose military skill might even have prevented European settlement of North America if not for devastating epidemics and disruption of the ecology? Where are the men and women who are today diligently struggling to assert their legal rights and express once again the value of their heritage?

The various Indian tribes of North America, like people everywhere, have a history that includes population expansion, adaptation to a range of regional environments, trade across wide networks, internal strife, and warfare. This was the reality. Europeans justified their conquests, however, by creating a mythical image of the New World and its native people. In this myth, the New World was a virgin land, waiting for the Europeans. The arrival of Christopher Columbus ended a timeless primitiveness for the original inhabitants.

Also part of this myth was the debate over the origins of the American Indians. Fantastic and diverse answers were proposed by the early explorers, missionairies, and settlers. Some thought that the Indians were descended from the Ten Lost Tribes of Israel, others that they were descended from inhabitants of the lost continent of Atlantis. One writer suggested that the Indians had reached North America in another Noah's ark.

A later myth, perpetrated by many historians, focused on the relentless persecution during the past five centuries until only a scattering of these "primitive" people remained to be herded onto reservations. This view fails to chronicle the overt and covert ways in which the Indians successfully coped with the intruders.

All of these myths presented one-sided interpretations that ignored the complexity of European and American events and policies. All left serious questions unanswered. What were the origins of the American Indians? Where did they come from? How and when did they get to the New World? What was their life—their culture—really like?

In the late 1800s, anthropologists and archaeologists in the Smithsonian Institution's newly created Bureau of American Ethnology in Washington,

8

D.C., began to study scientifically the history and culture of the Indians of North America. They were motivated by an honest belief that the Indians were on the verge of extinction and that along with them would vanish their languages, religious beliefs, technology, myths, and legends. These men and women went out to visit, study, and record data from as many Indian communities as possible before this information was forever lost.

By this time there was a new myth in the national consciousness. American Indians existed as figures in the American past. They had performed a historical mission. They had challenged white settlers who trekked across the continent. Once conquered, however, they were supposed to accept graciously the way of life of their conquerors.

The reality again was different. American Indians resisted both actively and passively. They refused to lose their unique identity, to be assimilated into white society. Many whites viewed the Indians not only as members of a conquered nation but also as "inferior" and "unequal." The rights of the Indians could be expanded, contracted, or modified as the conquerors saw fit. In every generation, white society asked itself what to do with the American Indians. Their answers have resulted in the twists and turns of federal Indian policy.

There were two general approaches. One way was to raise the Indians to a "higher level" by "civilizing" them. Zealous missionaries considered it their Christian duty to elevate the Indian through conversion and scanty education. The other approach was to ignore the Indians until they disappeared under pressure from the ever-expanding white society. The myth of the "vanishing Indian" gave stronger support to the latter option, helping to justify the taking of the Indians' land.

Prior to the end of the 18th century, there was no national policy on Indians simply because the American nation has not yet come into existence. American Indians similarly did not possess a political or social unity with which to confront the various Europeans. They were not homogeneous. Rather, they were loosely formed bands and tribes, speaking nearly 300 languages and thousands of dialects. The collective identity felt by Indians today is a result of their common experiences of defeat and/or mistreatment at the hands of whites.

During the colonial period, the British crown did not have a coordinated policy toward the Indians of North America. Specific tribes (most notably the Iroquois and the Cherokee) became military and political pawns used by both the crown and the individual colonies. The success of the American Revolution brought no immediate change. When the United States acquired new territory from France and Mexico in the early 19th century, the federal government wanted to open this land to settlement by homesteaders. But the Indian tribes that lived on this land had signed treaties with European governments assuring their title to the land. Now the United States assumed legal responsibility for honoring these treaties.

At first, President Thomas Jefferson believed that the Louisiana Purchase contained sufficient land for both the Indians and the white population. Within a generation, though, it became clear that the Indians would not be allowed to remain. In the 1830s the federal government began to coerce the eastern tribes to sign treaties agreeing to relinquish their ancestral land and move west of the Mississippi River. Whenever these negotiations failed, President Andrew Jackson used the military to remove the Indians. The southeastern tribes, promised food and transportation during their removal to the West, were instead forced to walk the "Trail of Tears." More than 4,000 men, woman, and children died during this forced march. The "removal policy" was successful in opening the land to homesteaders, but it created enormous hardships for the Indians.

By 1871 most of the tribes in the United States had signed treaties ceding most or all of their ancestral land in exchange for reservations and welfare. The treaty terms were intended to bind both parties for all time. But in the General Allotment Act of 1887, the federal government changed its policy again. Now the goal was to make tribal members into individual landowners and farmers, encouraging their absorption into white society. This policy was advantageous to whites who were eager to acquire Indian land, but it proved disastrous for the Indians. One hundred thirty-eight million acres of reservation land were subdivided into tracts of 160, 80, or as little as 40 acres, and allotted tribe members on an individual basis. Land owned in this way was said to have "trust status" and could not be sold. But the surplus land—all Indian land not allotted to individuals—was opened (for sale) to white settlers. Ultimately, more than 90 million acres of land were taken from the Indians by legal and illegal means.

The resulting loss of land was a catastrophe for the Indians. It was necessary to make it illegal for Indians to sell their land to non-Indians. The Indian Reorganization Act of 1934 officially ended the allotment period. Tribes that voted to accept the provisions of this act were reorganized, and an effort was made to purchase land within preexisting reservations to restore an adequate land base.

Ten years later, in 1944, federal Indian policy again shifted. Now the federal government wanted to get out of the "Indian business." In 1953 an act of Congress named specific tribes whose trust status was to be ended "at the earliest possible time." This new law enabled the United States to end unilaterally, whether the Indians wished it or not, the special status that protected the land in Indian tribal reservations. In the 1950s federal Indian policy was to transfer federal responsibility and jurisdiction to state governments, encourage the physical relocation of Indian peoples from reservations to urban areas, and hasten the termination, or extinction, of tribes.

Between 1954 and 1962 Congress passed specific laws authorizing the termination of more than 100 tribal groups. The stated purpose of the termination policy was to ensure the full and complete integration of Indians into American society. However, there is a less benign way to interpret this legislation. Even as termination was being discussed in Congress, 133 separate bills were introduced to permit the transfer of trust land ownership from Indians to non-Indians.

With the Johnson administration in the 1960s the federal government began to reject termination. In the 1970s yet another Indian policy emerged. Known as "self-determination," it favored keeping the protective role of the federal government while increasing tribal participation in, and control of, important areas of local government. In 1983 President Reagan, in a policy statement on Indian affairs, restated the unique "government is government" relationship of the United States with the Indians. However, federal programs since then have moved toward transferring Indian affairs to individual states, which have long desired to gain control of Indian land and resources.

As long as American Indians retain power, land, and resources that are coveted by the states and the federal government, there will continue to be a "clash of cultures," and the issues will be contested in the courts, Congress, the White House, and even in the international human rights community. To give all Americans a greater comprehension of the issues and conflicts involving American Indians today is a major goal of this series. These issues are not easily understood, nor can these conflicts be readily resolved. The study of North American Indian history and culture is a necessary and important step toward that comprehension. All Americans must learn the history of the relations between the Indians and the federal government, recognize the unique legal status of the Indians, and understand the heritage and cultures of the Indians of North America.

The Lenape creation myth, drawn by 20th-century artist William Sauts Bock, in which the Creator, Kishelemukong, built the world on the back of a giant turtle and created women and men from trees that grew on its back.

THE PEOPLE
OF
LENAPEHOKING

They are all free by nature, and will not bear any domineering or lording over them." So wrote a Dutch observer in 1655 about the Lenape (len-AH-pay) Indians and their neighbors. Fierce independence was always a characteristic of Lenape life. For most of their history they have struggled to put the needs of the individual before the requirements of custom and law and have worked to strike a balance between new ideas and old traditions.

The Lenapes were once sovereign over a vast domain stretching along the Middle Atlantic coast from New York Bay to Delaware Bay, between the Hudson and Delaware river valleys. They called their homeland Lenapehoking— "Land of the Lenapes." In their language, their name most properly means "ordinary people" or "common people." They are also sometimes known as Lenni Lenape, which translates roughly as "we, the people." Lenapes have always thought of themselves as members of a single ethnic group sharing a common sense of identity and heritage. Despite this sense of ethnic unity, they have been politically united as a single people only rarely in their history.

When the first European colonists settled on their lands in the early 1600s, there were between 8,000 and 12,000 Lenapes, according to conservative estimates. Most recent studies, however, strongly indicate that their population was probably twice as large. The Lenapes at that time were divided into as many as 20 different groups variously referred to as bands, villages, or tribes. Traditional Lenape social and political life has always been organized around a complex but flexible network of closely related independent communities. When Europeans first meeting these Indians asked who or what they were, they usually would identify themselves as inhabitants of a particular place, members of a certain family, or followers of an influential leader. Thus, place names such as Manhattan, which means "island," had social and political as well as geographical significance.

Many Lenapes believed that their history began when Kishelemukong, the Creator, brought a giant turtle up from the depths of a great ocean. The turtle grew until it became the vast island now known as North America. The first men and women sprouted from a tree that grew upon the turtle's back. Kishelemukong then created the heavens, the sun, the moon, all animals and plants, and the four directions that governed the seasons. Three of these directions were known as grandfathers; the fourth, who blew the warm winds of spring from the south, was known as "our grandmother where it is warm."

Many Lenapes believed that gambling among their grandparents of the four directions caused the seasons to change. Thus, spring came when South Grandmother was defeating North Grandfather, and autumn signaled a change in his luck. The seasons repeated themselves over and over. As in a game, however, the exact time of their appearance was always a matter of chance.

Most of those Europeans believed that the Lenapes and other Indians originally came from Asia. Most Lenapes, for their part, believed that their ancestors had come to Lenapehoking from the west sometime in the distant past. Archaeological evidence in the form of stone tools, clay pots, and other remains indicates that ancestors of the Lenapes came to the Middle Atlantic region nearly 3,000 years ago. Oral traditions, linguistic evidence, and ar-

chaeological remains from more recent sites suggest that the Lenape way of life observed by the early colonists developed more than 1,000 years ago. In addition to archaeology, comparative linguistics, and the Lenapes' own oral accounts, other sources of information about their past include documents written by the Europeans who visited and settled along the Middle Atlantic coast of North America. Where direct documentation for the Lenapes is lacking, the known practices and oral traditions of neighboring groups provide clues.

When Europeans first came among them, most Lenapes lived in bustling communities made up of one or more bark- and grass-covered longhouses or round wigwams. Their life centered around the close bonds of kinship and family. All rights to land and livelihood were held by the family, and people's sense of identity came from their family membership. Clans, or groups of related families that traced their origins to a common ancestor, served as links among relatives living in different communities.

Clan membership was passed down through succeeding generations of women, and every person belonged to the same clan as his or her mother. This type of clan system, in which kinship is traced through the mother's family, is called a matrilineal descent group, or *matrilineage*. All members of a person's father's family, including the father himself, were considered in-laws. Lenape matrilineages held all rights to

Traditional Lenape community drawn by 20th-century artist John T. Kraft. People are constructing a longhouse, tending gardens (in the background), and performing other daily tasks.

households and clan lands. Thus women, who tended to the fields, longhouses, and wigwams of Lenapehoking, owned those lands and lodges in trust for their clan. Another practice, which anthropologists call *matrilocality*, required a newly married husband to move in with his wife's family. This custom enabled women from the same clan to stay together on the same land over the course of a number of generations.

It has been widely thought that the Lenapes were divided into only three tribal clans ever since John Heckewelder, a Moravian missionary who lived among them from 1754 to 1813, confused three Lenape tribal names with what are believed to have been their principal matrilineages. Thus, all "Unamis" living along the Delaware River were thought to have belonged to the Turtle clan, all "Wunalachticos" of the seacoast to the Turkey clan, and all "Monsys" of the highlands to the Wolf clan. Today, most scholars agree that these names are most commonly regarded as only three of a much larger number of now-extinct matrilineages.

The Lenapes lived in a varied land of ocean beaches, vast marshlands, deep forests, fertile river valleys, and rocky highlands. Their land provided all the necessities of life. What little their land did not provide they obtained peacefully by trade, claimed from relatives by right of kinship, exchanged as gifts, or seized in wars with people from other areas.

The Lenapes lived by growing corn, beans, and squash; by tending small tobacco plots; by hunting deer, bear, and other animals; and by fishing and collecting wild foods. They made their tools, weapons, and sacred objects from stone, wood, bone, horn, shell, and sinew. Using these tools and materials, Lenape people built homes, fashioned dugout canoes, and crafted bows, arrows, bowls, spoons, and other implements.

They made their clothes from tanned deer and elk hides. Men wore breechcloths made from a long piece of deerskin worn between the legs and folded over a belt like an apron in the front and in the back. Women wore wraparound skirts. Both sexes wore belts or sashes, leggings, and light, soft-soled mocassins. Many Lenapes preferred to wear as little clothing as possible during the summer, and all went bare chested in warmer months. During the long winter months, they wore warm fur robes and blankets.

They decorated their clothing with shells, seeds, paint, stones, and

A fragment, or sherd, from a clay pot found in the upper Delaware River valley. The piece is sculpted in the shape of a face.

brightly dyed porcupine quills. They also decorated their bodies with paint, and many painted or tattooed images of guardian spirits or totem animals on their faces and bodies. Most Lenapes spread a lotion made of bear's grease, sunflower oil, or nut oil on their bodies to keep warm in winter and protect them from sunburn all year round. They removed all their body hair, and most young men and warriors shaved the hair off their head as well, leaving only a small, highly decorated scalp lock running down the center of their skull. All women and most older men, however, wore their hair long.

Men carved wooden implements and made stone tools and weapons. Disk-shaped and tubular shell beads and carefully crafted clay and stone tobacco pipes played important parts in sacred ceremonies and political meetings. Women wove grass, reeds, and cords made of braided strips of bark into mats and baskets. They made containers for food and other items out of elm and chestnut bark. They dug clay from riverbanks and hillsides and formed it into slabs, then pressed the slabs into gourd molds to form pots and bowls. They also rolled clay into long strips which they coiled and layered to form the sides of pottery vessels that were then smoothed and polished. They stamped, engraved, or pressed distinctive geometric designs and an occasional image of a human face into the soft wet clay. They also pressed cord-wrapped paddles, corncobs, or nets onto the wet clay to form other designs. They dried the pottery in the sun and fired it in fire pits to produce light and durable ceramic vessels.

Lenape life followed the seasons. Every spring Lenapes living along the coast came together in large camps near waterfalls and rapids. There they trapped, netted, or speared shad, salmon, herring, and other migratory fish swimming upriver. Other Lenapes living farther inland gathered in smaller camps to collect wild strawberries, hunt deer, or surprise bears as they sluggishly

Lenape people work together to catch and smoke-dry fish in order to build up their winter stores of food.

emerged from their dens after their long winter hibernation.

As spring edged into summer, many Lenapes moved to small communities located on rich soils, where they planted crops of corn, beans, and squash in garden clearings hacked from the forest with stone axes. Fallen trees and brush were gathered together or burned where they lay. Crops were then planted in the ash-enriched ground between the stumps. During this time, other people stayed at the seashore gathering fish and shellfish or making shell beads. At their villages and camps, Lenapes prayed for abundant harvests and other blessings during community ceremonies and in private rituals.

Summer was given over to tending crops, gathering berries and other wild foods, fishing, and hunting deer, elk, bear, smaller mammals, turkeys, and waterfowl. Summer also was the time for trading and for raiding. Evidence from archaeological sites and historical records documenting journeys of adventurous men and women to the Car-

Many Indian people used stones like these to grind corn into meal and flour. After many years of use, the large mortar stone would become hollowed out; the small pestle, rounded and smooth.

olinas and the Mississippi Valley suggests that Lenape traders, hunters, and warriors were accustomed to traveling long distances in search of game, goods, and adventure.

In autumn, Lenape people harvested and dried their crops. Drying preserved much of the food supply for the winter. They cut squash into strips and braided the husks of corn or the stems of beans together and hung them to dry in the autumn sun. Then they stored their harvest in the rafters of their houses, in wooden cribs, or in deep bark- or mat-lined pits. They cooked corn and beans together to make succotash. They prepared corn in a variety of ways—mixed with water to make hominy and with various other ingredients to make other dishes. Hundreds of deer, bear, and other animals were taken during fall communal hunts. Large groups of men and women surrounded a section of forest and set fire to the trees to drive the animals toward the spears and arrows of waiting hunters. As many as several thousand acres of woodland might be burned during these hunts.

At the approach of winter, people returned to their longhouses or wigwams in the heart of their respective territories. Congregating in council houses or sitting around cooking fires, they feasted upon the bounty of the preceding year, told stories, sang of their visions and exploits, and danced in thanksgiving long into the night. At various times small groups of hunters left the warmth of their homes to travel to remote camps. There they hunted deer and hibernating bears or trapped beaver, muskrat, otter, and other fur-bearing animals. Most people, however, stayed at home during the winter months. They worked, played, and prayed together until the warm spring winds and rains restored the green abundance of their woodland home.

The annual rhythm of the Lenapes' year was reflected in the cycle of their lives. Assisted by experienced midwives, most Lenape women gave birth to their children in small huts. Mothers carrying newborn babies on cradleboards could frequently be observed hard at work in the fields soon after childbirth. Babies were lovingly cared for. Dried moss and other soft, absorbent materials were used as diapers. When taken outdoors, infants were tied to cradleboards worn on their mother's back. The cradleboard might also be hung on a branch, where swaying breezes would lull the infant to sleep while the mother performed daily chores close by.

Children were greatly desired and loved. They deeply respected their elders and generally returned the affection bestowed on them. Strong words, gentle guidance, and the strength of example rather than force were used to correct behavior. Most youngsters began helping with chores as soon as they were able. Boys and girls learned their life skills through a combination of instruction, imitation, and play.

Young men and women sought spiritual power from dreams and

An early-20th-century Delaware cradle-board. Mothers carried their baby in a cradleboard, strapped to their back, while they performed their chores. Traditional cradleboards had strips of leather, instead of a wooden bar, as on this one, to protect the infant.

visions as they grew to adulthood. The passage from childhood to adult life was ceremonially recognized in special rituals for young men and women. Following these ceremonies, which in some cases could last for several months, young adults moved away from their parents' homes into the households of a mother's brother or sister. There they were taught the skills of adulthood by aunts, uncles, and other relatives.

Courting was an elaborate ritual of love songs, secret messages, and night meetings under blankets. Affection was shown openly among Lenapes, and there was no sense of guilt or shame associated with sexuality. Sacred myths dealt frankly with the subject, and even ordinary stories were filled with humorous sexual adventures. Sexual relations among courting couples and other unmarried people were not usually condemned, although venereal diseases, introduced to the Lenapes by Europeans, would ultimately put a damper on such behavior. Sex had many meanings to the Lenapes, and among unmarried Lenape people it was not confined to courting relationships only. But such activity came to an end following marriage. Sexual fidelity was considered an essential part of the marriage bond. Young people tended to marry early in Lenape society.

Most Lenape marriages were monogamous. Newlyweds customarily moved in with the wife's mother's family. Weddings joined together families as well as spouses. The birth of the first child usually sealed the union between marriage partners and their families. So strong were these bonds that frequently a Lenape man whose wife had died would marry one of her sisters in order to maintain close connections with kinfolk.

Particularly influential or wealthy men, however, could afford to be married to several women at the same time.

Marriages of one man to two or more sisters were especially common. Men often married several women from different clans or villages as well. The practice, known as polygyny, wherein a male may have more than one mate, increased the status of powerful men while establishing important social and political ties between different families. Women's labor was highly valued, and Lenape men were required to move into the households of their various wives. The women owned most property and spent much of their time raising children, cooking, and farming.

Jealousy tended not to be a serious problem in polygynous marriages. The respect Lenapes customarily showed one another discouraged rivalry, and the relationship among the wives in a household was generally harmonious. Divorce, however, was common in Lenape society. Inability of partners to live together and failure to have children were leading causes of separation. The act of divorce itself was simple. A man would announce his intention to separate from his wife and then go to live with relatives. A woman would place her husband's possessions in a pile outside the door of their house. The divorced husband simply gathered up his belongings and moved back into the household of his mother or other close relative. After a divorce, children always remained with their mother's family.

Disputes over property rights were rare. William Penn, the founder of Pennsylvania, would note in the 1680s that the Lenapes' "wealth circulateth like the Blood . . . though none want what another hath, yet [they are] exact Observers of Property." Although women owned much of the property, men owned other items such as their weapons and personal sacred objects, which they kept if their marriage ended.

The sexual division of labor in Lenape society was most sharply drawn among young married adults. Young women were encouraged to gather wild foods; develop their skills as potters, basket makers, and embroiderers; become mothers; and tend to household duties such as cooking, housekeeping, and gardening. Young men helped their elders around the house and in the fields. When they left their villages, they followed the path of the hunter, the trader, and the warrior. Especially talented young men and women inspired by dreams or visions were trained by elders specializing in the spiritual and healing arts to be *meteinuwak*—that is, "doctors" or "medicine people."

After the childbearing years, specific sexual roles lost importance as both women and men of ability and experience rose to positions of leadership and responsibility. Leading by example and ability to influence public opinion, these elders guided the political, economic, spiritual, and social affairs of their people until death carried them off into the next world.

The dead were mourned bitterly. Loved ones were buried with their fa-

Lenape women performed specific chores, including shelling and grinding corn, collecting wild plant foods, and making moccasins.

vorite possessions. The merit of the dead could be measured by the length of time and the sincerity with which they were mourned. Mourners sometimes blackened their faces for an entire year. Thereafter, custom required that the name of the dead be uttered only under special circumstances. It was said that Lenapes invented new words rather than mention a common animal or thing if it was part of a dead person's name.

Many Lenapes believed that the souls of the dead traveled to a beautiful place along the starry path that is now called the Milky Way. Each star was believed to be the footprint of a ghostly traveler. Arriving in their paradise in the sky or beyond the horizon, the dead remained happily and eternally joined with their ancestors.

Membership in a Lenape matrilineal clan was determined at birth and never changed. Villages, tribes, and confederacies, in contrast, were more or less temporary collections of kin, friends, and neighbors. Led by a civil chief known as a *sakima* during peacetime and a war chief during periods of hostilities, these larger social and political groups formed whenever significant issues of peace, trade, or war arose involving people beyond the family circle. Both sakimas and war chiefs were advised by councils of elders and other respected members of the community.

In Lenape society, men were responsible for particular tasks, including removing trees and breaking up the ground to prepare the soil for cultivation.

The egalitarian nature of their society enabled the Lenapes to respond flexibly to changing conditions. Egalitarianism did not, however, mean total equality. Chiefs, medicine people, skilled craftspeople, warriors, and other exceptional individuals were recognized and respected for their abilities. Social standing and political achievement did not entitle anyone to order anybody else around. On the contrary, individuals inheriting special rights or acquiring special skills were expected to use them for the common good. Generosity was expected from those who had more, and those who possessed power soon lost it if they refused to share its benefits.

Decisions were made collectively by these cooperatively independent people. William Penn wrote, "'Tis admirable to consider, how Powerful the Kings are, and yet how they move by the Breath of their People." Any people who disagreed with particular policies were free to move to another community or to form one themselves. Sakimas governed by the power of persuasion rather than the persuasion of power. Although the status of chief was inherited from one's mother's clan, overbearing or incompetent leaders quickly lost both their authority and their followers to more capable and popular chiefs.

Although much is known about the Lenapes' politics and society, little is known about their inner spiritual life. Early accounts by European observers, however, clearly show that Lenapes, like all other tribal peoples, lived in a world charged with supernatural intensity. All things were thought to be alive, animated by spirits called *manetuwak.*

A robe, made of bearskin, and a mask, made of wood, that were worn by a mesingholi-kan *dancer during Lenape ceremonies. Dancers participated in such rituals to honor spirits in hopes that they would assist them in hunting and other activities.*

Manetuwak and all other beings were created by Kishelemukong, the Creator, "who creates us by his thoughts." Most Lenapes did not, however, believe that Kishelemukong was directly involved in everyday life.

Men and women looked for guidance and power from all manetuwak through dreams, visions, and prayer. During sacred ceremonies, dancers called *mesinghholikan* wore masks and dressed as game spirits known as *mesingw* and as other powerful supernatural beings. At these times the Lenapes called upon the power of supernatural forces or expressed thanksgiving for their blessings. The Doll Dance was one of the few ceremonies that continued to be celebrated into the 20th century. It is said that the Doll Being, Ohtas, first came to the people when a child made a cornhusk doll for a dancing companion. It was soon found that the doll possessed great healing powers. Afterward, Lenape families carved wooden Ohtas and held Doll Dances yearly to honor the Doll Being and bring prosperity and good health to their people.

All major transitions were marked by appropriate prayers, rituals, and ceremonies. Dances were held to honor the appearance of the first fruits in the spring, the green corn of summer, and the fall harvest. Earnest prayers welcomed the newborn into the world, blessed newlyweds, and bid farewell to the dead as they began their journey into the next world.

Meteinuwak possessing unusually powerful spiritual abilities directed these and other ceremonies and saw to the spiritual needs of Lenape people. People visited by guardian spirits, recovering from severe illness, or showing evidence of blessings from healing spirits repaid their supernatural bene-

A carved-wood Lenape Doll Being, Ohtas. The spirit was revered because of its healing powers.

The Lenapes spoke a language belonging to the widespread Algonquian linguistic family, one of the major groupings of languages in the world. Spoken by such diverse peoples as the Cheyennes and Blackfoots of the Great Plains and the Shawnees, Abenakis, and Ojibwas of the northeastern forests, Algonquian languages could be as different as English and Farsi, two members of the Indo-European language family. The Lenapes and their immediate neighbors spoke languages belonging to the division of the Algonquian linguistic family known as Eastern Algonquian, spoken by coastal peoples from the Carolinas north to the Canadian provinces of Nova Scotia and New Brunswick.

One early European chronicler described the sounds of the Lenape language as "sweet and full of meaning." William Penn wrote that "their Language is lofty, yet narrow . . . in Signification full; one word serveth in the place of three." There may have been as many as four dialects of Lenape, whose speakers usually had some difficulty understanding one another.

Two dialects of the Lenape language, Munsee and Unami, are still spoken today by a few elders. *Munsee* means "People from Minisink" (which in turn means "the stony country"). Munsee was originally spoken by people who lived in the rugged uplands of the lower Hudson and upper Delaware rivers. Unami, the dialect of the "Downriver People," was originally spoken by Lenapes who lived upon the

factors by becoming doctors and healers themselves. Others used their powers to cast spells, look into the future, or influence the course of events. Whatever their message or mission, however, religious leaders have exerted great influence throughout the often turbulent history of the Lenape people.

flat plains of the Atlantic coast and around Delaware Bay in what are now southern New Jersey, southeastern Pennsylvania, and northern Delaware.

The Lenapes have long lived in a complex social and political environment in which names often signify different roles and values. For this reason, the Lenapes and their descendants have been known by a number of different names during their long history. Many neighboring Eastern Algonquian–speaking people who regarded the Lenapes as ancestors or experienced elders frequently addressed them respectfully as "Grandfathers." Other Algonquians living to the west of the Appalachian Mountains referred to the Lenapes and other Eastern Algonquian Indians as Woapanachke— "Easterners." The French of Canada, for their part, often called many of these same people Loups, meaning "Wolves."

Iroquois Indians living between Canada and Lenapehoking spoke languages belonging to a completely different linguistic family, and therefore they knew the Lenapes by other names. Many Iroquois called the Lenapes Akotshakane—"Stutterers"—after the way the Lenape language sounded to them.

Dutch, Swedish, and English colonists moving into Lenapehoking during the 1600s knew the Lenapes and their neighbors as "River Indians." The English named one of these rivers the Delaware after Thomas West, baron De La Warr, who was the first governor of Virginia Colony. The name *Delaware* later came to be applied to all Indians living along the river's banks.

In the 1680s, William Penn said of the Lenapes that "in Liberality they excel, nothing is too good for their friend." Their generosity of spirit was as characteristic of the Lenapes as their strong individualism.

Respect for individuality always requires social and political flexibility. Too much flexibility, however, can lead to chaos, whereas too little is tyranny. Lenape survival has depended upon an extraordinary ability to find a middle way between these possibilities. In the process, they created a society intensely responsive to individual needs and desires. The respect accorded individual Lenapes by family members and fellow tribespeople in turn encouraged them to act loyally and responsibly toward their own communities. Traditions of tolerance, respect, and flexibility thus created a generally harmonious society relatively free of crime and discord. These traditions helped the Lenapes survive the shock and stress of European invasion followed by 200 years of dispossession, poverty, and exile.

Their descendants, today's Delaware and Munsee Indians, continue to carry on these traditions. Driven from their homeland more than 200 years ago, they are now scattered throughout the United States and eastern Canada. Their original territory is now part of the United States. Western Connecticut, southern New York, eastern Pennsylvania, and all of New Jersey and

Delaware occupy their ancient homeland. Most Lenapes who live on their ancestral lands are regarded as legal residents of their respective states, and all Lenapes living in the United States or Canada are citizens of their respective nations.

Separated by vast distances and divided by international borders, most descendants of the Lenapes continue to recognize a common identity and history marked by hardship and struggle. The story of their survival is a testimony to the strength of their traditions. It is also a testimony to the human will not just to survive but to preserve a unique sense of identity and purpose in a changing and often hostile world. ▲

Lenape family of the lower Delaware Valley, drawn in 1654 by Swedish engineer Peter Lindstrom. Contrary to the drawing, Lenape women did not dress in the same clothing as Lenape men.

EUROPEAN INVASION
1524–1664

Lenapes may have seen their first European when the Italian navigator Giovanni da Verrazano, employed by Francis I, king of France, sailed along the eastern coast of North America in 1524. More frequent contacts began in 1609, when Henry Hudson, an English navigator in Dutch employ, sailed up the river that now bears his name. At the same time, the Frenchman Samuel de Champlain was traveling south from what is now Canada, on the lake later named for him, towards the Hudson River. Farther south, in Virginia Colony, settlers had been living for two years in the first permanent English community, Jamestown.

These explorers and colonists were soon followed by more Europeans—merchants, administrators, soldiers, and settlers. Within a few years, the Lenapes were surrounded by growing numbers of strangers from another continent.

They called these strangers Shouwunnock, or "Salty People." The name most likely refers to the settlers' origins on the other side of the great salt ocean.

It may also reflect the settlers' bitterness towards the Lenapes and all others different from themselves. Some Lenapes say that this name refers to their myth about the origin of the white people. Those holding this belief say that white people were created from the foam of the salt water beating upon the shores of Europe and that they then floated west to the shores of Lenapehoking.

The Europeans were driven by visions of power and wealth. Many were drawn by the promise of ruling over a wilderness empire rich in resources. Others dreamed of winning quick wealth in the fur trade by giving the Indians glass and metal trinkets in exchange for valuable pelts and skins. Many colonists saw the Indians themselves as potential sources of wealth in the form of laborers for their farms and fields. Still others dreamed of finding gold, silver, and other precious metals in the mountains and riverbanks. Attracted by the prospect of riches for the taking, Dutch, English, French, and Swedish merchants and explorers flocked to the region. They quickly built

Italian explorer and navigator Giovanni da Verrazano, who was the first European known to have visited the Lenapes in the early 16th century.

trading forts and settlements in and around Lenape territory during the early 1600s.

The Dutch government, the United Netherlands, awarded a group of merchants the right to colonize the heart of the Lenape homeland in 1614. Organized as the Dutch West India Company, this corporation established a series of strategically located trade forts throughout the area by 1626; the colony officially became the province of New Netherland in 1623. The Dutch traders built their main forts along what they called the North (later the Hudson) River. Fort Amsterdam, erected at the southern tip of Manhattan Island, provided a deepwater port, which made it possible for full-sized ships to carry supplies, trade goods, and news between continents. The city of New Amsterdam (later New York City) sprang up around this fort. Fort Orange (later the city of Albany) was strategically established one hundred miles inland. Located at the junction of what are now called the Hudson and Mohawk rivers, Fort Orange gave the Dutch control of the lucrative fur trade in the north. To the south, the Dutch erected small forts and settlements along the South River (today called the Delaware), in what are now the states of Pennsylvania and Delaware.

South of Lenapehoking, meanwhile, the English were expanding their colony at Jamestown, and to the north they were establishing settlements on Massachusetts Bay. Still farther north, French colonists in Canada founded Quebec, Montreal, and other towns along the St. Lawrence River. Sweden also attempted to establish a colonial empire, New Sweden, along the South River in 1638. There they traded with the Lenapes and the Susquehannocks, a neighboring Iroquoian-speaking tribe, until 1655, when Dutch troops captured the posts and claimed the land for the Netherlands.

The Dutch conquest of New Sweden dramatically illustrated the competition among the colonists. The colonizing nations of Europe were locked in a struggle for control of eastern North America that would end only when the colonists attained their independence in 1783. Divided by conflicting national loyalties, each colony pursued its own policies. Colonial societies were further segmented into political parties, religious sects, business enterprises, social classes, and other contending factions. Conflicts frequently cut across national and cultural boundaries, and some were so bitter that colonists sometimes collaborated with foreign enemies to gain advantages over their own countryfolk. Partisan colonists also enlisted Indians in their political struggles and wars throughout this era.

Despite their divisions, the Europeans soon established thriving settlements throughout the Northeast. Although settlers did not discover gold, they did find a rich trade in exchanging their metal tools, guns, glass beads, and textiles for the Indians' furs. The promise of wealth attracted growing numbers of settlers to the Middle Colonies of New York, New Jersey, Pennsylvania, and Delaware. There were only 5,000 Europeans in the region in 1650. There would be more than 750,000 by the time of the War of Independence in 1776.

At the time of the first European contact, the Lenapes were divisible into

East and West Indiamen, *an etching made by Dutch artist Reiner Nooms in the 1750s. West Indiamen brought Dutch traders, soldiers, and settlers to Lenape territory.*

A 1640 etching of New Amsterdam, capital of the Dutch colony of New Netherlands. The English renamed the city New York in 1664.

essentially two major groups: those to the northeast, who spoke Munsee (or in some cases, Mahican), and those to the south, who spoke Unami. These two divisions were in turn divided into smaller communities, from which many present-day locales derive their names.

Northernmost among the first group were the Catskills and Wappingers, and directly below them the Esopus (River Indians). Below the Esopus lived the Manhattan Indians, of New York Bay; the Hackensacks, of northern New Jersey; and the Minisinks, of northern Delaware. Some tribes dwelling on Long Island also spoke Munsee. Among these were the Rockaways, the Massapequas, and the Canarsees, to the west; and the Matinecocks and Unchachaugs, to the east.

The southern group of Lenapes—in southern New Jersey, southeast Pennsylvania, and Delaware—diverged not only in speaking Unami; their social organization also differed from their northern neighbors. These Unami-speakers dispersed themselves into a large number of small, independent villages. Among the better known of these were the villages of Sanhikan, Rancoca, and Narraticong, in southern New Jersey; the villages of Playwicky, Passayunk, Tulpehocken, and Ockehocking, in southeast Pennsylvania; and the villages of Quenomysing, Minguannan, Shackamaxon, and Sickoneysinck, in Delaware.

The Indian population, including that of the Lenapes, dropped drastically during the 1600s. Alcohol, introduced by the colonists, shortened many lives through abuse. Thousands perished in wars with other Indians and with the Europeans. Many more were killed by smallpox, measles, malaria, and other terrifying diseases brought to North America by Europeans. Smallpox and malaria are deadly wherever they occur, but because the Indians had never been exposed to measles they had no immunity to this malady. As a result, they suffered greatly from diseases that were less often fatal to Europeans.

The Lenapes may have experienced at least 14 epidemics between 1633 and 1702. One observer wrote that not one-

COLONIZATION OF THE NORTHEAST, 17th AND 18th CENTURIES

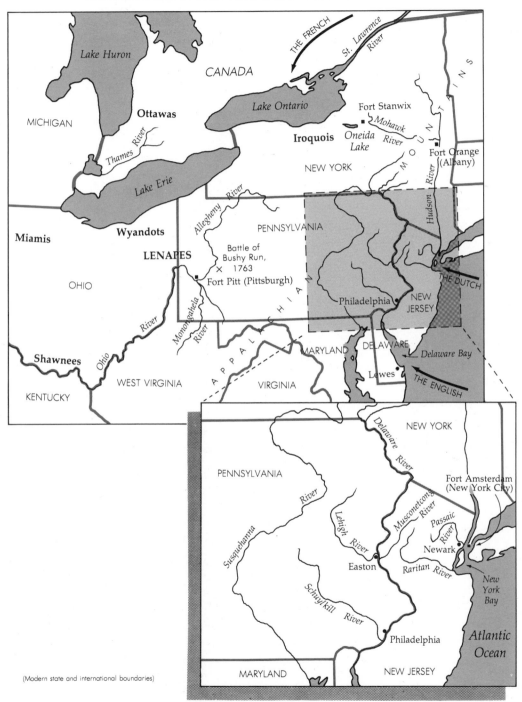

(Modern state and international boundaries)

tenth, or even one-thirtieth, of their 1609 population was alive in 1679. Thus the Lenape people, who may have numbered 24,000 before the Europeans arrived, dwindled to probably fewer than 3,000 by the year 1700.

Despite such alarming population losses, Indians throughout the region were forced to compete with one another as well as with Europeans for survival as their lands and resources disappeared. Contending tribes fought to monopolize access to trading posts or control of trapping grounds and trade routes. By exchanging furs, Indians were able to obtain goods they could not produce themselves: guns,

wool blankets, copper pots, and iron knives and hatchets. Only those with such advantages could feed their families and protect themselves as their rivals increased in strength.

The Lenapes' location initially gave them a certain advantage in this competition. Their beaches were particularly rich sources of the clamshells used to make small, tubular, purple-and-white beads known as wampum. Produced in quantity after Europeans introduced metal drills that allowed quick mass production, wampum became a highly prized commodity in colonial and Indian communities. Indians, for their part, had long used shell beads for

Wampum belt believed to commemorate the 1682 Treaty of Shackamaxon between William Penn and the Lenapes. Considered spiritually significant by the Indians, wampum (shell beads) were used as currency by cash-poor Europeans in the colonial era.

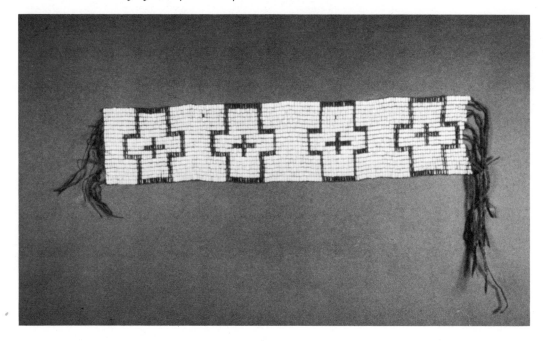

Metal ax heads. Metal goods, introduced to the Indians by Europeans, became very important during the colonial era because they were often more efficient and durable than the Indians' traditional stone tools.

sacred rituals and diplomatic maneuvers. Short of coins, Europeans soon used wampum as currency.

The Lenapes tried to exploit this resource. Working industriously, they manufactured millions of shell beads for trade. Their success in this effort, however, attracted unwanted attention from nearby tribes, who competed with Europeans in taking wampum from the Lenapes, often under threat of violence. Unable to resist their powerful neighbors, most Lenapes ultimately were forced to give away much of their wampum as tax or tribute.

Lenapes faced other economic problems in the mid-17th century. Their territory had never been a particularly favorable habitat for fur-bearing animals. The few beavers inhabiting the area were probably hunted or trapped to extinction by 1640. Needing beaver pelts and other skins to trade for increasingly important European-made goods, Lenapes turned to other territories and tribes for their furs.

Their trapping and trading parties ranged widely throughout the Northeast in search of pelts. They forged particularly strong relations with Indians

Thomas West, baron De La Warr, was governor of the colony of Virginia from 1610–11. The Delaware branch of the Lenapes, as well as the colony (now state) of Delaware, are named after him.

living in the fur-rich Ohio country. Many Lenapes, however, found their movements blocked by powerful tribes. To the south and west, the Seneca of the Five Nations and the independent Iroquoian-speaking Susquehannocks jealously guarded paths and rivers leading beyond the Appalachian Mountains to the rich trapping lands in the Ohio Valley. To the east, the Pequots stood between the Lenapes and abundant New England trapping grounds and well-stocked Boston traders. And to the north, the Mohawk and the Oneida of the Iroquoian-speaking Five Nations and the Algonquian-speaking Mahican and prevented competitors from gaining direct access to furs and French trade goods from Canada.

Lenapes responded to these challenges in different ways. Many moved nearer to the colonists' towns to take advantage of closer trade and social contacts. Others, such as those Lenapes who began moving in the 1600s to what is now Ohio, abandoned their ancestral lands. But most relocated to already existing Lenape villages farther inland, away from the main European settlements along the major rivers.

In the north, many Munsees moved away from New Amsterdam north to the rocky uplands east of the Hudson River. Others moved west from the Hudson up along the Esopus and Wallkill rivers below the Catskill Mountains. Farther south, Munsees living along the shores of Long Island Sound and the lower Hudson moved inland toward the rugged interior. Others moved eastward on Long Island to the Indian towns of Canarsee, Rockaway, Massapequa, and Matinecock in what are now Brooklyn, Queens, and Nassau County.

Between 1640 and 1700 Munsees living around New York Bay and the lower Hudson also moved south and west to villages along the Hackensack, Passaic, Raritan, and Musconetcong rivers in what is now northern New Jersey. During the first decades of the 18th century most of these people joined other Lenapes at Minisink towns along the upper Delaware River. It was there that they and their kinfolk first came to be known as Munsees, "People from Minisink."

By the 1630s, many Unami-speaking Lenapes living around the mouth of the Schuylkill River were driven east, into what became New Jersey, by Susquehannocks seeking to dominate the Delaware River trade. Most of these people settled along the many small creeks flowing through the Jersey pinelands. Most later moved north to central New Jersey or to the Lehigh River country above Easton, Pennsylvania, and farther west to Tulpehocken (Turtle Place) on the upper Schuylkill above Reading, Pennsylvania. Others later moved south of Philadelphia to communities located at Okehocking (Surrounded Place) on Brandywine Creek. These and other Unamis ultimately became known as the Delaware Indians, after the river running through the heart of their territories. The name itself springs, as previously mentioned, from Thomas West, baron De La Warr, the English soldier who as governor of Virginia Colony dissuaded settlers from abandoning Jamestown during a difficult point in their enterprise.

Many Lenape families who left Lenapehoking during the 1600s and 1700s moved away forever. Others left only temporarily. Many were lured away by the fur-rich trapping grounds, but others simply did not want to live near Europeans. The dispersal of the Susquehannocks by the Iroquois during the 1670s removed a major obstacle to Lenape travel to the west. By 1700 many

Lenapes had settled along the Susquehanna River valley to remain close to their ancestral homes. Others moved farther away, to Indian towns in the Allegheny and Ohio river valleys beyond the Appalachian Mountains, or north, where they were among the French and their Canadian Indian allies. A few may have gone even farther, into the deep forests north of the Great Lakes or west into the prairie grasslands of the Great Plains.

Although many Lenapes initially welcomed Europeans, others violently opposed them. In 1631, for example, the Sickoneysinck destroyed Swanendael (today the town of Lewes, Delaware), one of the first Dutch settlements along the South River. Others, such as the Munsees living along the lower Hudson River, were driven to open resistance only gradually.

Misunderstanding, miscalculation, and stupidity led to a wave of murders, assaults, and thefts by settlers and Indians alike during the 1630s. This ever-increasing violence finally erupted into war in the following decade. After being attacked without warning first by the Dutch and later by their Mahican allies, a confederacy of at least 12 Munsee communities went to war against the settlers. The resulting conflict, which lasted from 1640 to 1649, included a series of European massacres of Indian communities between 1643 and 1645. This phase of the fighting is today known as Governor Kieft's War, after the Dutch governor who, on February 23, 1643, ordered the massacre of

Wood engraving of Swedish and Lenape traders made in Sweden in 1702. The first Europeans in North America wanted little to do with Indians, and the historical inaccuracies of the engraving attest to this—the Indians' dwellings and headdresses are not Lenape.

Munsee refugees fleeing to New Amsterdam from a Mahican attack.

Another lower Hudson River Munsee confederacy went to war against the Dutch in 1655. The "Peach War"—named after the event which allegedly triggered it, the murder by a Dutch settler of an Indian woman who was picking peaches on his property—ended inconclusively after two years. Shortly thereafter, another war broke out farther upriver. Known as the Esopus War, after the major Munsee tribe fighting the Dutch, this conflict ravaged Indian and European communities throughout the mid-Hudson Valley.

The Esopus War ended only after the English seized New Netherland from the Dutch in 1664, renaming it New York. The Dutch had become so weakened by conflict with the Indians that their colony fell easily. Learning from Dutch mistakes, the triumphant English made peace the following year with all Indians in the region. English officials quickly invited the Indians living in New York to treaty conferences, where they heard out Indian complaints and concerns.

The peace was an illusory one, however, as many sources of conflict remained unresolved. Most of the Lenapes were pressed between the mountains and the coastal towns of the colonists. Powerful neighboring tribes fought to dominate or absorb them. English settlers from the Atlantic Coast continued to travel farther inland.

The Lenapes were now in a world wider than any their ancestors had known. European settlers had brought with them new ideas, useful tools, and undreamed-of wealth. But their firearms, alcohol, epidemic diseases, and insatiable appetite for land would continue to plague the Lenapes throughout the colonial era.

The Lenapes' wisest leaders realized that their only hope lay in buying time, which held the possibility of recovery for themselves and decline for their enemies. They bought that time by playing powerful rivals against one another. This struggle would dominate all aspects of Lenape life over the next two centuries. ▲

William Penn's Treaty with the Indians, *painted by American
artist Benjamin West in 1771. This work depicts Penn's 1682 meeting with representatives of the Delaware, Susquehannock, and Shawnee tribes. West obtained information about the event from his
father, Thomas, who was one of the founding members of the colony.*

UNEASY
NEIGHBORS

The wars of the mid-1600s devastated both the Indians and Europeans. Settlements throughout the region had been destroyed, and thousands of Lenapes and hundreds of Europeans killed. But the English, having conquered the Dutch, were determined to avoid their competitors' mistakes. By listening to the Indians' concerns and promising friendship and justice, English officials put an end to nearly 15 years of warfare with them.

In addition to these hostilities, many Lenape communities warred with other Indians during the colonial era. A number of Indian assaults upon Lenape towns are reported in documents of the period. There are, for example, records of attacks by Algonquian-speaking Pequots and the Iroquois League of Five Nations. The earliest attacks were probably economically motivated efforts to keep Lenapes away from trading and trapping grounds farther north and west. As the colonial era wore on, the attackers' motives became more political, as they attempted to conquer or dominate the Lenapes and their neighbors outright.

Weakened by disease and threatened on all sides, most Lenapes tried to accommodate their powerful English and Iroquois neighbors. Those remaining in Lenapehoking accepted the peace overtures of the English and became their close allies. Lenapes living further inland fell under the influence of the Iroquois Five Nation or of Mahican or Susquehannock rivals. After the Iroquois finally defeated and dispersed these rivals in the 1670s, the Five Nations claimed authority over all Lenapes.

During these years, growing numbers of independent-minded Lenapes joined their kinfolk west of the Appalachians in Ohio, or north in Canada. In both locations they entered the French sphere of influence. The French did not attempt to dominate the Lenapes living among them. They were absorbed in their own struggle with England for control of North America, and were more interested in trade than settlement. The Lenapes in Ohio established close relations with such French Indian allies as the Miamis, Ottawas, and Shawnees. Those in Canada be-

41

Etow Oh Koam, King of the River Nation, *a 1710 painting by John Verhelst. The River Nation was composed of Mahicans and Munsees living along the Hudson River.*

came closely associated with the Schaghticokes, Caughnawagas, Abenakis, and other Indian refugees from New York and New England.

Lenape communities located between major European settlements generally maintained a surprising degree of independence. Indians living in the Raritan River country of central New Jersey, between Manhattan and Philadelphia, and those in the Esopus River

country, between New York City and New England, took advantage of the intense rivalries dividing the colonial governments. Frequently switching loyalties, the Indians would play contending provinces against one another.

Most Lenapes, however, simply protected their own interests by allying themselves with their closest neighbors. Those near Manhattan cultivated the friendship of New York traders, landowners, and provincial officials. Those farther north established ties with New Englanders. Those to the south, along the lower Delaware River, looked for allies in New Jersey or Pennsylvania. And all Lenapes living near Iroquois people struggled to accommodate the Five Nations.

This complex system of interlocking alliances uniting Indian tribes and colonies throughout British North America became known as the Covenant Chain, after the agreements, or covenants, among the involved parties. Membership in this alliance provided important benefits to the Lenapes. First and foremost, Covenant Chain allies provided military protection against the French and their Indian allies to increasingly weak Lenape communities. Covenant Chain allies could also make available better and more plentiful trade goods while providing limited legal and political safeguards for Lenape lands, lives, and livelihoods. Colonial authorities tended to deal justly with Covenant Chain Indian allies so long as their demands did not conflict with government policies.

Membership in the Covenant Chain could not, however, assure complete protection or guarantee a secure future. Most colonists believed that Indian rights should be respected only until they had "the heathen on better terms," in the words of one settler. It is likely that even the most trusting Indian must have had strong doubts about the reliability of such allies.

Lenapes knew what their powerful neighbors thought of them and probably had similar feelings about their allies. But wise Lenape leaders were acutely aware that they needed protection in an increasingly dangerous and uncertain world. At the very least, these alliances meant survival. They also allowed the Lenapes to replenish their dwindling numbers while they bided their time in the vain hope that the English and Iroquois might destroy themselves in war or disappear in some mystically induced fire, flood, or other cosmic disaster.

Protection came at a high price. As junior partners in the Covenant Chain, the Lenapes frequently had to tolerate public insults and humiliations from their allies. Originally addressed as "brethren," Lenape elders came to be called "children" by colonists at Covenant Chain meetings. Iroquois diplomats also sometimes treated them rudely and occasionally called them "women" at treaty councils. Even today, many Lenapes cannot forget the scathing words of the Iroquois Canasatego at a Philadelphia treaty council in 1742, as he ordered the Lenapes off land claimed by Pennsylvania. Speaking in the name of the Iroquois League, he called the Lenape men dishonest and greedy, "Lewd Women [who] receive the Embraces of Bad Men . . . We don't give you the liberty to think about it. You are Women; take the advice of a Wise Man and remove immediately."

Lenape elders could occasionally turn such harsh insults to their own advantage. In 1709, for example, Minisink chiefs politely refused to let their warriors join the English against the French, saying, "they were only Squas and no fighting men."

English goods commonly traded to Indians for beaver pelts. "One beaver pelt could be traded for any of the following: 2 silver crosses, 6 small brooches, 24 bells, . . . 8 knives, or 2 hatchet heads," according to a 1795 trade standards guide used by European traders.

Insults were the smallest part of the price Lenapes paid for protection by their Covenant Chain allies. As the Minisink chiefs found, Lenapes were often expected to provide warriors for English and Iroquois military adventures. The Lenapes were also expected to provide strategic information and furnish food and labor to their allies. English authorities required them to trade only with English merchants, accept English prices, and obey English laws when visiting their settlements. Although these merchants frequently cheated them, Lenape traders found English goods generally cheaper, sturdier, and more attractive than those offered by the French. English laws often protected their lives and property as well.

English records, however, also clearly show that the Lenapes were expected to peacefully sell their lands. Between 1630 and 1767, Lenape people put their marks upon nearly 800 deeds, conveying nearly the whole of Lenapehoking to the Europeans. Most deeds recorded legitimate transactions of relatively small tracts for mutually acceptable prices. Some, however, such as the 1737 "Walking Purchase" of lands to the west of the Delaware River, fraudulently deprived the Lenapes of hundreds of square miles of ancestral territory.

The Walking Purchase derived its name from the unusual provisions of the transaction. In the early 1730s, William Penn's sons, who had inherited Pennsylvania Colony after their father's death in 1718, were near bankruptcy. They desired to buy land from the Lenapes at a low price to resell at a handsome profit, but the tribe would not cooperate. Then, in 1736, the Penn brothers produced an earlier deed, which gave them claim to the amount of land that could be walked in one and a half days from a point in lower Bucks County due north. Trusting colonial courts to look the other way, the Penn brothers first cut a road through the previously virgin territory, then hired professional runners to span the distance. One runner permanently injured himself in his exertions, and the Penn brothers ended up with more than twice the land the Lenapes had expected to relinquish.

The Walking Purchase took virtually all of the remaining Lenape lands in eastern Pennsylvania, and the loss left an impression upon Delawares that has not yet entirely disappeared. More than a few scholars suspect that anger over the Walking Purchase was a major reason the tribe later joined in the war against the English.

The Indians and colonists held different views of land ownership and use. Most Lenapes believed that land was a gift from Kishelemukong, the Creator, held in common by all of the occupants. Europeans generally regarded land as private property to be bought and sold. Both Lenapes and Europeans, however, did have a number of surprisingly similar ideas about land. Both believed, for example, that they held land as custodians for spirit

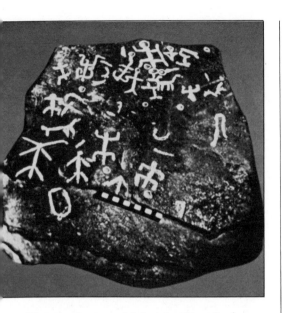

Pictographs carved into a boulder. Such engravings often depict human, animal, and abstract figures.

beings. Lenape clans held land in trust for Kishelemukong, whereas European monarchs held it by "divine right." Both peoples also used complex systems to transfer land rights. Europeans used deeds, licenses, and other documents. The Lenapes did the same with unwritten but equally binding oral agreements recorded by wampum belts and pictographs—symbols drawn on bark or rock. And both peoples ritually exchanged valuable gifts to finalize their land transactions. The only difference was that Lenapes used trade goods, whereas Europeans used money to seal their bargains. Influential Lenape leaders probably did not fully comprehend the meaning of the first deeds they signed during the 1630s. The large

number of deeds they and others signed in later years, however, clearly indicates that most Lenapes came to understand and accept European land tenure concepts after their first dealings with settlers.

The overwhelmingly powerful Europeans paid the present-day equivalent of many thousands of dollars in gifts, goods, and money over more than 150 years to acquire undisputed title to the lands of a far weaker people. Europeans were clearly too strong, and their demands for land too great, to be denied by the Lenapes or any other Indian group. Colonists nevertheless preferred peaceful and orderly land acquisition to violent seizure. Land grabs caused wars, which were expensive and uncertain in outcome. Laws regulating the acquisition of Indian territory, however, established a more or less efficient system whose sole purpose was to peacefully and effectively take land from Indians and place it firmly in European hands.

The Lenapes faced a dilemma. Land was everything to them. Yet the Europeans clearly wanted all of it. How could they appease Europeans without losing everything? Wiser Lenape leaders, with their time-honored traditions of subtlety, moderation, and compromise, did their best to slow down land transfers. Whenever possible, Lenape leaders steered European purchasers away from their lands to those of other tribes. For example, in 1663, the Hackensack chief Oratam, explaining that his elders did not want to sell their lands near Newark, New Jersey, told prospective Dutch purchasers that better lands were available in Esopus country. Knowing that the Esopus were then at war with the Dutch, Oratam broadly hinted that it might be easier and cheaper to seize their lands than to force reluctant allies to sell inferior lands closer to home. Oratam's ploy evidently worked, as the Dutch never did buy the Hackensack lands.

Such stratagems did not always succeed. When purchasers insisted on acquiring land, Lenape leaders did their best to limit the area they were forced to sell and restrict it to less desirable locations. They further delayed being evicted from lands already sold by using the European legal system. Although they did not fully understand the intricacies of the law, they did know enough to tie things up in court. Exploiting the widespread knowledge

that Indians were often victims of land fraud, Lenape leaders often challenged the legal validity of deeds to their lands. Taking advantage of unclear wording and vague boundary descriptions, they also played rival landowners against one another. Years passed before some conflicts were resolved; one dragged on in the courts for more than 50 years, through the American Revolution.

Other Lenapes learned to manipulate European land laws to further their own people's interests. They transformed Indian deeds from simple contracts into legal devices approaching the status of treaties—often allowing them continued hunting and fishing rights on the land, or continued possession of land while cases dragged on in court.

Such leaders, both men and women, were able to attract great numbers of followers. Seen as cooperative by colonial authorities, they were also

A deed, or bill of sale, on which marks of two Lenape women attest to their sale of land.

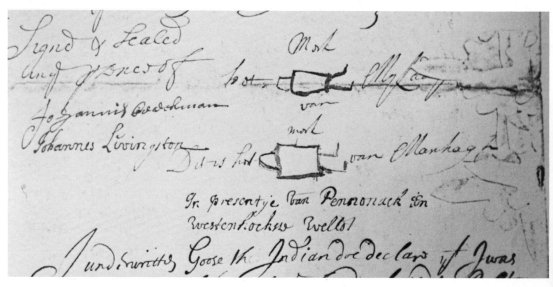

able to increase their influence among Europeans. In this way, Lenape leaders such as Oratam and Sassoonan, who repeatedly affixed their marks to Indian deeds, were more than mere figureheads. They safeguarded their people's life and property under extremely difficult conditions.

Over time, such leaders came to be chosen by a consensus of both the Lenapes and the colonists. In early Pennsylvania, for example, the power of the near-legendary chief Tammamend was enhanced by his 1683 treaty of friendship with William Penn (1644–1718), Quaker founder of that colony. (Tammamend, celebrated for his wisdom and virtue, would become the namesake of New York City's Tammany Hall political organization in the 1800s.) As the colony grew, so did its power, and Tammamend's successor, Sassoonan (also called Olumapies), would rule through the tacit consent of Pennsylvania authorities. Although they did not appoint Sassoonan, it was their recognition of him as "king of the Delawares" which gave him authority and prestige for 30 years, until his death in 1747. When such recognition was withheld, a Lenape leader could expect trouble from his own people.

The difficulties Lenape leaders faced in dealing with colonial authorities are illustrated by the career of Pisquetomen, Sassoonan's strong-willed and articulate heir. Pisquetomen, alarmed and angered by colonial expansion, was unable or unwilling to hide his contempt for Europeans. Pennsylvania au-

thorities mistrusted him and refused to recognize his authority. This rejection effectively prevented him from developing a significant following among his own people. Ultimately the Delawares submitted the name of his brother, Shingas, for approval by the Pennsylvania authorities.

Oratam's heir, Pierwim (known to colonists as Hans), made the wrong friends at the wrong time. He tried to consolidate his position in New Jersey by selling land only to New Yorkers who claimed New Jersey for themselves. This angered and alienated his colonial New Jersey neighbors. Resisting New York's attempt to absorb their province, New Jersey colonial officials took their revenge against Pierwim by buying land only from his Indian rivals. In so doing, they effectively undermined Pierwim's influence among both colonists and his own people. Within a few years Pierwim was isolated and living in relative obscurity.

Most Lenape leaders, however, were able to deal more effectively with the colonists for a while. Through compromise and diplomacy, they did their best to hold the Europeans back. But it was an uneven struggle, and in the end the Lenapes were forced to give up everything and leave their lands. Superior numbers rather than superior skill defeated them. It would take all their skill, however, to see the Lenapes through the trials and tragedies that awaited them on their long journey into exile beyond the western horizons of Lenapehoking. ▲

*Delaware leader Teedyuscung, "He who makes the earth tremble,"
by 20th-century artist William Sauts Bock.*

CAUGHT BETWEEN GREAT POWERS

New waves of European immigrants swept into Lenapehoking during the first half of the 18th century, forcing most Lenapes into western exile in the Susquehanna and Ohio river valleys by 1750. The French and Indian War (1754–63) hastened this process. Only a few Lenapes would remain on their ancestral lands by 1800.

Relations with their neighbors became increasingly more difficult for those Lenapes who remained in their homeland in the early 1700s. Weakened by war and disease, increasingly dominated by other tribes, and living on lands wanted by colonists, Lenapes found themselves no longer protected by their Covenant Chain allies. Only the most extraordinary leaders could protect their people's interests against the inroads of the colonists and the Iroquois.

Weequehela, known to his contemporaries as the "Indian King of East New Jersey," was such a leader. Living among European settlements, he and his people struggled to come to terms with their white neighbors. Weequehela was the son of an important sakima, and many of his brothers were chiefs of Lenape villages between Delaware Bay and New York Bay. The name *Weequehela*, which means "weary" or "exhausted," was given to him as an adult as a humorous nickname playing upon his unusual energy, resourcefulness, and ambition. Weequehela respected the traditions of his ancestors. He also, however, adopted many European customs. He is known, for example, to have dressed in the high style of the period—breeches, linen shirts, and buckled shoes—and lived in a wood-frame house containing fine china and elegant furnishings. He also was said to have been an owner of black slaves and a bootlegger of illicit alcohol as well as a mill operator. An influential leader, he often successfully defended his people in colonial courts against charges of theft, assault, and murder. Land was evidently often part of the price of justice. On May 11, 1715, for example, Weequehela signed a deed

49

handing over Lenape land to colonists on the same day that two of his people were acquitted of murder charges.

Records indicate that Weequehela signed more than 20 deeds relinquishing portions of his people's remaining lands in Monmouth and Middlesex counties, New Jersey, between 1675 and 1716. Though he evidently sold some land for political purposes, Weequehela complained that he had signed other deeds after being made drunk by his white neighbors. In 1727, a year marked by tensions that nearly led to war between Indians and colonists, Weequehela finally lost patience with his greedy neighbors. While in a drunken rage, he killed a land speculator named Samuel Leonard during a violent argument over a particularly unjust land transaction. After surrendering himself to provincial authorities, Weequehela was quickly tried and hanged. His followers were outraged by the execution of their protector, and most left New Jersey for the Lehigh River country shortly after his funeral.

Demoralized and distressed, many other Indians left Lenapehoking voluntarily during these years. Still others were forced out. Moving from settled farmsteads, most adopted the more nomadic life practiced by the trappers, traders, and warriors of the tribes west of the Appalachian Mountains. Those staying behind gradually lost their property and became nomads in their own land.

Many Lenapes settled in or near reservations of a few hundred acres of poor land such as Ockehocking, south of Philadelphia. Others moved to remote and inaccessible swamps, pine barrens, or mountain ridges. Unable to make a living farming their small plots, they traveled from one place to another gathering food, hunting game, and visiting relatives. Many worked for colonists as farm laborers and servants, or sold homemade splint baskets, straw brooms, and herbal remedies. Others found employment with the whaling fleets and merchant vessels that sailed from colonial ports such as New York and Boston.

Hundreds joined mission communities. Missionaries had been in the region since the early 1600s, working with little success to convert Lenapes and other Indians to Christianity. They had better results during the 1740s, when they built new mission communities in and around Lenapehoking. The more prominent of these were established at Stockbridge, Massachusetts; Schagticoke, Connecticut; Cranbury, New Jersey; and around the forks of the Delaware River at Bethlehem, Pennsylvania. Worsening economic conditions compelled many Lenapes to move to such settlements.

Many of these missions were established by Moravian Protestants. The Moravians, who had fled from persecution in Europe in the early 1700s, were a communal, peace-loving sect particularly sympathetic to the Indians. Other missions were founded by less tolerant Presbyterian preachers during a wave of Protestant religious enthusi-

Moravian missionaries baptizing Christian Indian converts. The Moravians left Europe in the early 1700s to escape religious persecution.

asm called the Great Awakening, which thrived from around 1740 to 1750. Despite their differences, both sects gained acceptance by preaching in the Indian languages, tolerating those customs not in direct conflict with Christian teachings, and banning liquor. Many missionaries also fed, clothed, and sheltered needy visitors; taught reading, writing, and crafts; and, like powerful chiefs, defended their followers in colonial courts.

Many Lenapes welcomed help from the missionaries, who had come during turbulent years. France and England fought several wars for control of eastern North America between 1689 and 1762. Both sides constantly tried to enlist Indians. Lenapes served the French and English alike as warriors, scouts, and laborers; many never returned from their service. Others died when their villages were attacked and burned by invading armies and bands of raiders. More than half of all Lenapes died or fled their homeland between 1689 and 1697, during just one of these wars.

Disease continued to take a heavy toll. Many hundreds of Lenapes died in a particularly devastating series of epidemics of smallpox and malaria between 1679 and 1702. Many more died in later outbreaks.

As war and disease weakened the Lenapes, tens of thousands of English, Scotch-Irish, and German settlers flooded into their land, openly defying colonial laws that protected Indians. Some stole Lenape property, raped Lenape women, and assaulted and occasionally killed Lenape people. Terrorized or disgusted, most Lenapes left their homeland to join relatives in the west.

Most made new lives in the western country. Although many welcomed relief from the pressures of constant contact with Europeans, they were unable to completely avoid political involvement with their new neighbors. Lenapes moving to the Susquehanna Valley country, for example, found themselves living upon land claimed by the Iroquois. The Iroquois had adopted their Tuscarora kinfolk when the latter fled North Carolina in 1722 following defeat in a colonial war. Thereafter the Iroquois were known as the Six Nations. Now they tried to dominate the Lenapes, Shawnees, and Nanticokes, and sent overseers to live among these Indians and administer their affairs.

Farther west, in Ohio, Lenapes established their own towns or lived among independent-minded Shawnees, Miamis, and Wyandots. They gradually settled together in villages along the Tuscarawas and Muskingum rivers. They could not, however, escape Europeans entirely. In Ohio, the Len-

George Washington as a young man, wearing his colonial Virginia militia uniform.

apes and their neighbors entered the French sphere of influence. French-Canadian missionaries, traders, and government agents frequently gave the new immigrants food, firearms, tools, and clothing. These presents helped win the Indians' friendship as the French prepared for their final showdown with the English for control of eastern North America.

As war grew imminent, the scattered Lenapes living far from home among strangers developed a renewed sense of national identity. Those from the northern reaches of their former homeland began calling themselves Munsees; those from the southern part of Lenapehoking began calling themselves Unamis.

Every Lenape community experienced profound change during these years. Influenced by the colonists' way of life, increasing numbers of Lenapes chose, for example, to build log cabins rather than traditional bark longhouses. Wooden rail fences surrounded their homesteads and fields. Formerly unacquainted with domestic animals, many Lenapes now raised chickens, horses, hogs, and cattle. Large cornfields and orchards of apple, cherry, and peach trees were planted. Now riding on horseback as frequently as they had paddled canoes, many Lenapes also traveled west to the Great Plains and beyond to trade muskets, lead, gunpowder, and the latest style in European tools, textiles, and ornaments for the furs, horses, and buffalo hides of the Plains tribes.

French and English competition for control of this trade had flared into open conflict many times. The final chapter of this struggle began in a small field in western Pennsylvania in the early summer of 1754. Guided by Lenape and Iroquois scouts, a young Virginia militia colonel named George Washington had been sent west with an expedition to halt French expansion into the upper Ohio Valley. He began by ambushing a small French patrol near what is now Pittsburgh. A larger French unit forced the English colonials to retreat to the south. Washington and his men quickly erected a small wooden stockade, which they named Fort Ne-

cessity, in an open field known as the Great Meadows. It was there, on July 4, 1754, that Washington surrendered his vastly outnumbered force and marched back to Virginia.

Lenape warriors fought on both sides during the opening battles of this war. Angered by the English failure to protect their interests, most Lenapes awaited an opportune moment to abandon their Covenant Chain allies and join the French. They made the break a little more than a year after Washington's defeat, when a small force of French and Indians (including several Lenapes) destroyed a large English army and killed its commander, General Edward Braddock, at the new French stronghold of Fort Duquesne, not far from Fort Necessity.

The decision to fight the English changed Lenape life forever. Those Lenapes who joined the French cut themselves off from the Covenant Chain. They no longer had much to lose by doing so; cooperation with their former allies had already cost them their homeland. A French alliance held the promise of strength and security to the embittered Lenape people. They were not alone in this sentiment; after Braddock's defeat most Indians sided with the French against the British and their Iroquois allies. By going over to the French, the Lenapes also defied their Iroquois overlords and symbolically shed the "petticoats" the Six Nations had placed upon them.

Lenape leaders realized that their tribe's survival required independence from other powers as well as unity among themselves. Lenapes living in scattered settlements throughout Ohio formed a nation under the leadership of powerful chiefs such as Shingas, Beaver, and Netawatwees. The new nation was buoyed by waves of religious enthusiasm. The Delaware prophet Neolin preached that Lenapes who returned to the old ways would find spiritual redemption. Moravian missionaries, on the other hand, also attracted many new Lenape converts, who preferred to give up the old ways for new lives as Christians. Whatever their beliefs and affiliations, however, most Lenapes came to informally agree on one thing by 1755: They would no longer be just Lenapes—"people." They would be Delawares, an independent nation. And they would never again easily trust strangers. Instead, they would look to their own warriors and elders for guidance and strength.

As an independent people, the Delawares sent their warriors east with Shawnees, Wyandots, and others to attack the English. Delaware war parties ambushed unwary travelers and struck isolated homesteads as far east as New Jersey. They killed hundreds of settlers. Many women and children were taken back to Ohio as captives. Delaware raids rolled the line of settlement back to eastern Pennsylvania as panic-stricken colonists abandoned their farms and fled to shelter in the English forts that sprang up all over the Pennsylvania, New Jersey, and New York frontiers.

Encouraged by the success of their raids on the English, the Delawares were in no mood to discuss peace terms. When the Iroquois asked them to lay down their arms in a 1758 conference, a defiant Delaware delegation replied, "We are men, and are determined not to be ruled any longer by you as women." The French, however, were unable to provide adequate provisions or ammunition to their Indian allies. A successful British attack on the Delaware town of Kittanning, in western Pennsylvania, on September 8, 1756, further shocked the confident warriors. It was soon followed by other raids. Suddenly aware of French weakness, and unable to stop the English themselves, many Delawares began to turn their thoughts toward peace.

Not all Delawares had gone to war against the English, however. True to their new religion, Moravian Delawares refused to fight anyone. Others living among the English in New York, New Jersey, and the Susquehanna Valley country also attempted to remain neutral. Eager to stay out of the war, many of these Delawares chose an obscure chief named Teedyuscung to be their spokesman.

Teedyuscung was a Moravian convert who ultimately abandoned his Christianity to return to traditional beliefs. He was also an eloquent orator.

The New Jersey–born Teedyuscung took over the Delaware leadership from a chief named Nutimus just as the war against the English was breaking out. Nutimus, as leader of the New Jersey

Indians living in eastern Pennsylvania, had vigorously resisted Pennsylvanian attempts to take away his people's lands under the fradulent misuse of the Walking Purchase treaty. William Penn's secretary, James Logan, had attacked Nutimus as having no right to Pennsylvania. Nutimus disagreed, saying, "the Indians [do] not consider the river as any boundary, for those of the same nation [live] on both sides of it." Besides, Nutimus asked, how did the European-born Logan come "to have a right here, as he was not born in this country?" But power prevailed in the argument. In the end, Nutimus's Iro-

quois allies had compelled him to submit to the Pennsylvanians' demands.

Teedyuscung took up the struggle for his people's welfare where Nutimus left off. Having lived among the colonists, he was aware of the bitter rivalries dividing them. He also knew that the English were terrified by the thought of an Indian war in the heart of their colonies. An astute diplomat, he took every opportunity to exploit these jealousies and fears by playing one faction against another.

Teedyuscung was also a political realist. He knew that the French were outnumbered by the British in North

A late-18th-century drawing of the Delaware town of Kittanning, Pennsylvania, destroyed by a British attack in 1756.

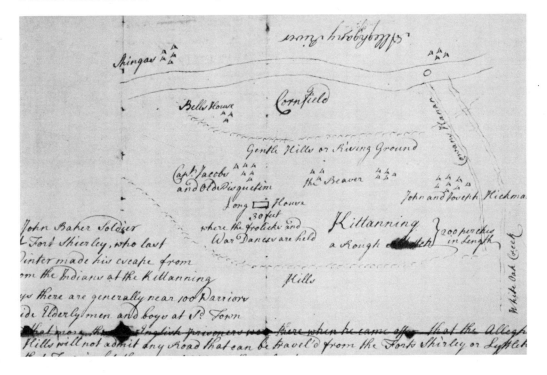

America and would not be able to protect their Delaware allies if the English colonists united. Realizing that continued hostility would ultimately cause the English to turn against all Indians, he worked to bring the Delawares and their Shawnee allies to the conference table.

Teedyuscung and other frontier diplomats took advantage of the growing sentiment for peace in the late 1750s to talk the Delawares and other tribes into meeting with the English. Serving as a mediator, Teedyuscung eventually brought representatives from most Delaware communities to a series of treaty meetings with the English held between 1756 and 1758 in the frontier town of Easton, Pennsylvania.

At Easton, the English promised peace, protection, presents, fair trade, and the return of Indian prisoners. They also told the chiefs that they would not take any more of their lands and promised compensation for ancestral territory. Backing up their promises with actions, New Jersey authorities paid the Delawares for all outstanding land claims in their state and created a small reservation at Brotherton for those wishing to remain in the province.

In return, the Delawares and other Indians were asked to cease fighting, adopt a position of neutrality, and give up their prisoners. They were also asked to allow English troops free passage through their territories. The English promised that their soldiers would leave once the French had been completely defeated. Though suspicious, the Delawares had little choice but to accept.

They soon learned just how important their cooperation at Easton had been to British war aims. Within weeks, British troops passed safely through Delaware country and, on November 24, 1758, captured the strategic Fort Duquesne, which was renamed Fort Pitt after the reigning English prime minister. (Ultimately the site would evolve into the present-day city of Pittsburgh.) This vital position enabled the English to isolate and then capture most French outposts west of the Appalachians. The French held on in Canada for four more years, but finally surrendered eastern North America to England in 1763.

As the Delawares feared, the English did not leave their country at the war's end. Instead, their commander, Sir Jeffrey Amherst, announced that the soldiers would remain permanently to "protect" the Indians. Talk of war again flashed through the Delaware villages, but the chiefs were all too aware of their military weakness. At best, they could field 500 warriors at any one time. The English regularly assembled frontier armies of 2,000 to 3,000 soldiers. All the Ohio tribes together could have gathered twice that number, but they were not unified enough to do so. Despairing of ever being able to drive the English away by force of arms, many Indians turned to the spiritual world for help and to their prophets for counsel.

In the Tuscarawas River valley of Ohio, the Delaware prophet Neolin preached to his people that if they rejected European goods and ideas and returned to the ways of their ancestors, the Great Spirit would drive away the whites. Many Delawares accepted Neolin's message. Unfortunately, he also called on Delawares to give up their metal arrowheads, guns, knives, and hatchets, which placed them at a distinct military disadvantage.

Neolin's message spread rapidly among the tribes. Pontiac, an Ottawa war chief from Michigan, was particularly impressed. Pontiac was both a practical leader and a deeply spiritual man. He differed with Neolin on the use of firearms and weapons and urged all Indians living west of the Appalachians to unite to drive the English away. Traveling widely throughout Ohio country, he found supporters in every tribe. Pledging to fight and die together, they waited for their moment to strike.

The moment came sooner than most expected. Angered by Lord Amherst's policies and the English failure to withdraw, Pontiac gave the order to attack shortly after the war officially ended in January of 1763. The warriors moved quickly and with ruthless efficiency, taking the English by surprise. Within weeks, they captured all but three of the western British posts. They soon besieged the remaining ones, at Forts Detroit, Niagara, and Pitt. By June, it looked as if the Indians would succeed in driving the English back east of the Appalachian Mountains. Once again, many settlers were killed or captured by Delaware and Shawnee war parties.

Outraged settlers exacted fearsome vengeance. Unable to strike at the raiders themselves, the settlers moved against the peaceful Indians who lived among them. During the winter of 1763, an armed band of several dozen marauding colonists known as the Paxton Boys (after the Paxton district—ironically, a Delaware name) rounded up and murdered peaceful Indians at Harrisburg, Pennsylvania. Encouraged by their success, they and their sympathizers threatened or attacked Indian people wherever they found them.

The aged chief Teedyuscung was also a victim of settler unrest on April 19, 1763. He had been living quietly in a log cabin built for him by the Pennsylvania government in the Susquehanna Valley village of Wyoming, near the present site of Wilkes-Barre, Pennsylvania. When settlers from New England illegally invaded his lands, Teedyuscung tried, along with the Pennsylvanians, to talk the New Englanders into leaving. Shortly thereafter, he lay dead in the ashes of his burned-down cabin.

Meanwhile, the hostile Delawares faced major difficulties; many were short of ammunition or suffered from smallpox or starvation. Despite these problems, the Delawares and their Shawnee allies kept Fort Pitt under siege throughout the summer of 1763.

Painting depicting the massacre of Indians in Lancaster, Pennsylvania. The Paxton Boys, a group of white men from the colony's Paxton district, killed the Indians in retaliation for raids by the Delawares, Shawnees, and their allies.

In August, however, English troops led by Colonel Henry Bouquet, a Swiss soldier serving the British, defeated a mixed force of Delawares and other Indians at the Battle of Bushy Run and relieved the post. Shortly afterward, other English columns attacked and burned most of the remaining Delaware towns in Pennsylvania and New York.

British troops moved west against the Ohio towns during the following year. Short of ammunition and weary after more than two years of continual war, the Delawares and their allies could not stop them. Capturing the important Delaware town of Coshocton in November 1764, Colonel Bouquet forced the Delawares to lay down their arms, give hostages as a guarantee of their good behavior, and return all prisoners.

This last provision, however, proved to be far more difficult than either the colonists or the Indians had anticipated. By the time the fighting finally ended in 1765, many captive colonist children had lived among the Indians for more than 10 years. Many had been adopted into the tribes and refused to return. Strong bonds of affection had grown between them and their adoptive Delaware parents. More than a few had reached adulthood, married Indian spouses, and now had children of their own. Considering themselves Indians, they did not want to return to what had become to them an alien and hostile society.

The Delawares and the other tribes, however, ultimately honored the promises they had made. Bringing their captives to Fort Pitt and other frontier posts, weeping Indian families led crying children or gently pushed sullen,

Indians returning captives in a 1764 drawing by American artist Benjamin West. Many whites developed close ties to the Indians who captured them.

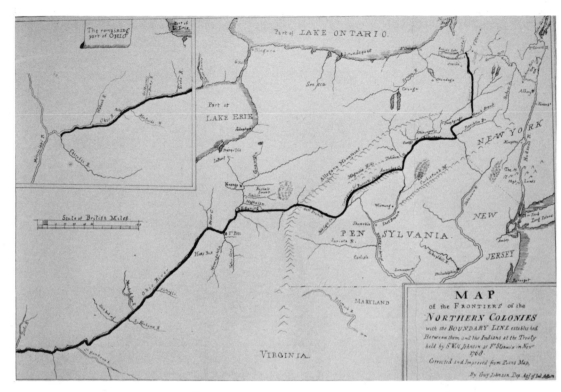

Map of northeastern North America showing the boundaries agreed upon by the British and Indians in the treaty of Fort Stanwix in 1768. The Indians retained the northern territory.

reluctant teenagers toward waiting soldiers, church officials, and families of settlers hoping to recognize and reclaim loved ones lost to Indian raiders.

On May 8, 1765, the Ohio and Pennsylvania Delawares signed a formal peace treaty with the English. The terms were harsh. The Delawares were forced, among other things, to accept any general frontier boundary demanded by the Iroquois and British leaders. This boundary line was finally drawn three years later, on October 22, 1768, by a treaty signed at Fort Stanwix,

near Oneida Lake in what is now New York State. Under the terms of the Treaty of Fort Stanwix, the Iroquois sold the Susquehanna Valley country, which was east of the Fort Stanwix line, to the English. Those few Delawares remaining there were forced to abandon their towns and move either north among the Iroquois or west to Ohio.

The French and Indian War had shattered the eastern Delaware communities. The survivors moved west to safer places. Only isolated remnants stayed behind in remote villages in the upper Susquehanna or mid-Hudson river valleys.

A few Delawares also remained in and around small, supervised settlements such as the Massachusetts Stockbridge mission and the 3,044-acre Brotherton reservation in the New Jersey pine barrens. (The Massachusetts reservation became such a center for these Indians that their descendants would go on calling themselves "Stockbridge-Munsee" even after they had forsaken the locale.) By the 1760s, however, virtually all Delawares were living in Ohio. This exile would strengthen their sense of nationhood. As a nation, they would stand together against those intent upon taking their lands. ▲

CHIEF WHITE EYES

LENAPE "INDIAN" CHIEF AND U.S. LIEUTENANT COLONEL COQUETAKEGHTON IN THE AMERICAN REVOLUTION • SAUTS •

White Eyes, a Lenape leader. He was probably the first Lenape to sign a treaty with representatives of the 13 colonies.

FROM
OHIO
TO
INDIAN TERRITORY
1770–1866

By 1770 most Delawares lived in towns along the Tuscarawas and Beaver rivers in eastern Ohio. They were a varied group. Munsees and Mahicans from New York, Unamis from the Delaware River valley, and Moravian Delawares from Pennsylvania all built settlements of their own. Having learned the importance of unity during the recent wars, they joined to form a Delaware nation. Netawatwees, of the Turtle clan, established the emerging nation's capital in the heart of the Tuscarawas River country at Newcomer's Town (a city that still exists today as Newcomerstown).

In 1771, Newcomer's Town was an expanse of orderly streets and nearly 100 houses, most made of logs. Its population was almost exclusively Lenape. Netawatwees lived in a comfortably furnished two-story house with a shingle roof, glass windows, and a stone chimney.

In the newly formed government, Netawatwees was advised by a Great Council, made up of representatives of all Delaware towns who were chosen on the basis of their matrilineal kinship groups. Only the Moravian Delawares were denied representation in council deliberations, because their Christianity made them suspect to their fellows. Most chiefs at Newcomer's Town tolerated the Moravians in the area. Many, however, neither fully accepted nor entirely trusted them, and several sought to drive them away altogether. At one point, these chiefs convinced the Great Council to send the noted warrior Glickhican (Gun Sight) to force the Moravians to leave. Engaging him in discussion, the missionaries talked Glickhican into joining their community instead.

Following their tradition of tolerance, the Ohio Delawares together built their new nation. By maintaining unity among themselves, they gained some authority in the region and earned the respect of their neighbors. It was probably at this time that these neighbors

63

began to address the Delawares respectfully as "Grandfathers" at public meetings and conferences with other tribes. The Delawares, weary of war, lived peacefully in their Ohio towns. Women continued to till large cornfields, tend the orchards, and raise horses, cattle, pigs, and chickens. Men continued to work as trappers and traders, now traveling farther north and west. Moravian missionaries, who had inaugurated European agricultural methods, also taught some modest industrial skills such as European loom techniques and metalworking. Moravians translated the Bible into the Delaware language, rendering it phonetically with the English alphabet. In order to read it and other books, many Moravian Delawares learned to read and write Delaware, German, or English.

This industrious peace was shattered when the 13 colonies revolted against British rule in 1775. The war brought to the surface the fundamental divisions within the Delaware nation. Their separate communities generally followed the political allegiances of the people they lived among. Many Munsees living among the Iroquois in New York, for example, remained loyal to the English. The Moravian Delawares, and many other Ohio Delawares, tended to favor the rebelling colonists.

The Delaware nation became increasingly divided as the war dragged on. Netawatwees' successor, White Eyes, supported the colonists. Named chief of the Delaware nation by the Great Council at Newcomer's Town in 1774, White Eyes is believed to have signed, sometime during the following year, the first treaty between an Indian tribe and representatives of the 13 colonies that would soon become the United States of America. It is thought to have been a simple treaty of friendship; the document itself has since disappeared. In a treaty signed at Fort Pitt on September 15, 1778, however, White Eyes clearly committed his people to a military alliance with the new nation. He may have been bribed with lavish gifts and a lieutenant colonel's commission in the Continental Army. He may also have been promised that the treaty would convince the Continental Congress to admit the Delaware nation into the union as the 14th state. Or the illiterate White Eyes may have been tricked into signing a document whose contents were misrepresented to him.

Soon after the treaty meeting broke up, American authorities announced White Eyes's death from smallpox. He had in fact been murdered by frontiersmen while returning to the Delawares' new capital at Coshocton, Ohio. Concerned that the news would turn the Delawares against them, the colonists covered up the murder. In the end it made little difference. Repeatedly attacked by marauding frontier settlers and tired of empty colonial promises of protection, arms, food, and supplies, most Munsees and many other Delawares soon joined the English.

(continued on page 73)

A CULTURE IN TRANSITION

As the Lenapes were forced by non-Indian settlers to leave their eastern homeland and move west, their way of life changed to harmonize with their new environments, neighbors, and circumstances. These changes in Lenape culture were expressed in their religious, ornamental, and functional objects.

The impoverished Lenapes who relocated to Indiana in the early 1800s no longer had the time or wealth to observe all of their ancient religious celebrations. Under the guidance of the prophet Beate, they consolidated them into a single annual ceremony—Xingwikaon, or Big House. For this ritual, celebrants made objects such as mesingw (game spirit) masks, turtle-shell rattles, and drums.

As the Lenapes continued to move farther west, they came into contact with Indians of the Plains. These groups influenced them to craft objects from silver. Once the makers of shell-bead wampum in their coastal homeland, the Lenapes now became adept silversmiths.

The materials and patterns the Lenapes used to decorate functional objects also changed. In the east, the tribe had decorated its clothing with porcupine quills colored with vegetable dyes. In the west, the Lenapes also began to use glass beads, often creating floral and abstract designs similar to those used by their new Indian neighbors.

A Lenape wooden flute, dating from the late 19th or early 20th century.

A carved wooden mask of a mesingw, *or game spirit, worn by a dancer in the Big House ceremony.*

A Big House prayerstick, topped by a mesingw head and strung with metal chimes and janglers.

A Big House rattle, made from the shell of a box turtle and filled with bits of marine shell.

A Big House drum and drumsticks carved with mesingw. The faces have been hewn so that they look toward the drummer.

Lenape silver armbands, probably from the late 19th century. Such items were introduced to North America by non-Indian settlers in the 1600s but were later made by Indians.

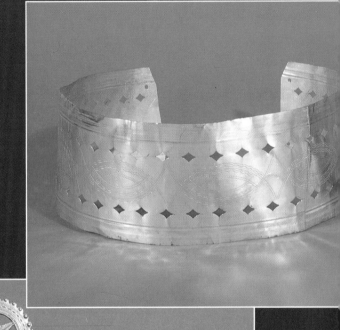

Silver brooches were worn by Lenape women to adorn their cotton dresses, which gradually replaced traditional animal skin clothing.

Hair ornaments such as this were worn by Lenape men in the West. Feathers or ribbons were attached to the small wand, which protruded from the hair.

Three bracelets and a ring crafted in the late 19th century by a skilled Lenape silversmith.

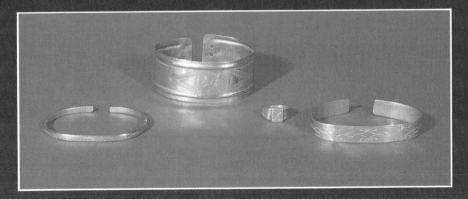

A Delaware shirt adorned with beads in designs much like those used by tribes native to the Midwest.

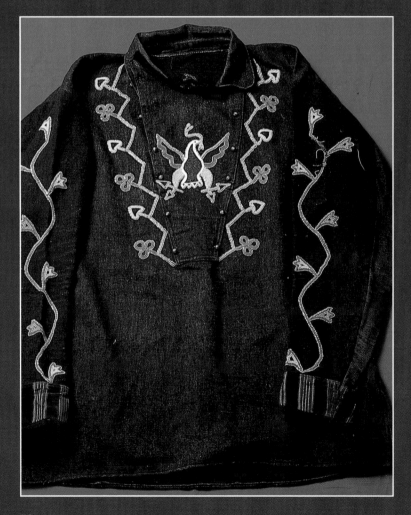

70

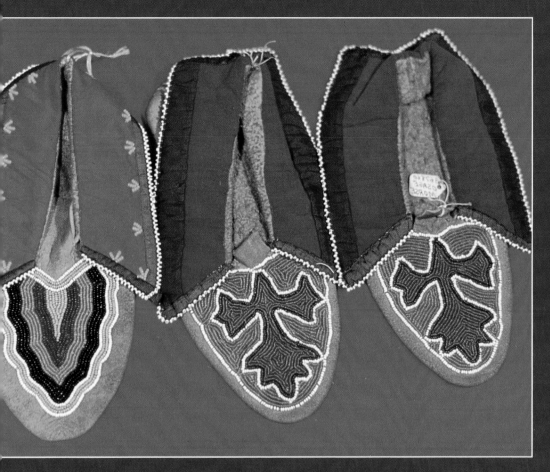

Colorful, abstract beadwork patterns decorate the tops and flaps of these Delaware moccasins from the early 20th century.

This Delaware shoulder bag, crafted in Oklahoma in the early 20th century, is made of deerskin decorated with dyed quills.

Delaware war leader Buckongahelas, with mesingholikan dancer, as drawn by 20th-century American artist William Sauts Bock.

(continued from page 64)

For the third time in as many decades, chiefs such as Captain Pipe and Buckongahelas led Delaware and Shawnee warriors in raids on the frontier settlements. Soon, American army columns began to move against Indian villages. In 1779, George Washington sent three American armies, under the overall command of General John Sullivan, into the heart of the Iroquois Nation. Their orders were to destroy all Iroquois towns and fields. The westernmost of these armies, commanded by Colonel Daniel Brodhead, advanced north from Fort Pitt to attack and burn Iroquois and Munsee villages along the Allegheny River. Farther east, Sullivan's column, marching into Iroquois country, destroyed the last of the Delaware towns along the Susquehanna.

Three years later Brodhead led another army, this one containing many Delawares, into the Ohio Valley country. The presence of friendly Delaware troops did not keep the American soldiers from murdering captives or burning and plundering Coshocton and other Ohio Delaware towns. This campaign would be remembered thereafter as a sad time when Delawares fighting alongside the Americans killed other Delawares who were defending their Ohio towns.

The Continental Army was not the only force attacking the Delawares. Frontier militiamen scoured the forests for Indian raiders. Hating all Indians, they killed most Delawares unfortunate enough to encounter them. One unit, led by Lieutenant Colonel David Williamson, committed perhaps the most brutal atrocity of the War of Independence. In March 1782, Williamson's company arrived at the pacifist Moravian settlement of Gnadenhutten. Accusing the Mahican and Delaware converts there of aiding the Indian raiders, the troops rounded up and systematically murdered all 90 of the town's inhabitants—men, women, and children—as they prayed and sang hymns. Glickhican was among the victims. The Gnadenhutten massacre outraged people on both sides of the Atlantic. Many Americans condemned Williamson's cold-blooded killings. Neither he nor any of his men, however, were ever charged with the crime.

England gave up the war and recognized American independence with the Treaty of Paris, signed on September 13, 1783. Once again, the treaty makers forgot their Indian allies, and both England and the United States re-fused to give up claims to the Ohio Valley. The English continued to occupy forts at Niagara and Detroit, and to provide arms and ammunition to Delawares fighting against the Americans. And American troops continued to protect settlers who now poured into Ohio.

Fighting between Delawares and Americans went on for nearly two years after the end of the revolution. Finally, the Delawares were able to make a separate peace with the Americans, at a heavy price, in the Treaty of Fort McIntosh, signed on January 21, 1785.

A 1797 lithograph of Miami war chief Michikiniqua, "Little Turtle." He led a confederacy of Indians, including many Delawares, that destroyed two American armies.

Forced to give up the Tuscarawas River country, most Delawares moved to western Ohio. But settlers had been inundating Tuscarawas River country even before the treaty had been signed, and shortly thereafter, they demanded the expulsion of all Indians from all of the Ohio Valley. The Delawares, banding together with 34 other tribes, prepared once again for conflict. The British supported this coalition with arms, ammunition, and supplies. Alarmed by the coalition's strength, the United States moved quickly to break up the alliance. Repeated diplomatic efforts failed. Because of the repeated atrocities they had suffered, the Delawares and their allies were in no mood to negotiate. Instead, Delaware warriors led by Buckongahelas defended their villages and attacked invaders.

Determined to crush the confederacy, the American government sent three armies into Ohio. The first, a force of around 1,500 men led by veteran commander General Josiah Harmar, was defeated in 1790 by warriors led by the Miami war chief Little Turtle. One year later, another army, led by the territorial governor, General Arthur St. Clair, was virtually destroyed. Finally a third army, specially trained to fight Indians by its commander, General Anthony Wayne, marched into Ohio and decisively defeated the warriors on the banks of the Maumee River at Fallen Timbers on August 20, 1794.

On August 3, 1795, the defeated Delawares and their allies gave up their remaining Ohio lands at the Treaty of Fort Greenville. Disgusted, many of the Delawares who had actively opposed American expansion moved as far away as possible from any lands claimed by Americans. Some moved west with Shawnees to towns along the Mississippi River below St. Louis in Spanish-held Louisiana. Others moved north to Canada. The main body of Delawares, however, continued to try to live near, cooperate with, and benefit from the Americans. Carrying their possessions in wagons or on their backs, they moved west to establish new settlements along the White and Wabash rivers in Indiana.

In Indiana the Delawares looked to the future with uncertainty and misgivings. They appreciated the fertile fields surrounding their White and Wabash river towns, such as Wapekommekoke (White River), Wapeminskink (Chestnut Tree Place), and what would become the present-day city of Muncie. But knowing how attractive such farmland was to Americans, most Delawares were certain that greedy settlers would soon come to claim their lands.

This time the Delawares felt there was no place else to go. Some of them had traveled through Indiana before as traders. They knew that beyond these newly plowed fields lay only bleak prairies, desert wastelands, or dark, trackless forests. They knew too that poor and warlike tribes lived in these barren places.

Moreover, the Indiana Delawares were now poor themselves. Nearly a half-century of warfare had taken its

DELAWARE MIGRATIONS, LATE 18th TO MID-19th CENTURIES

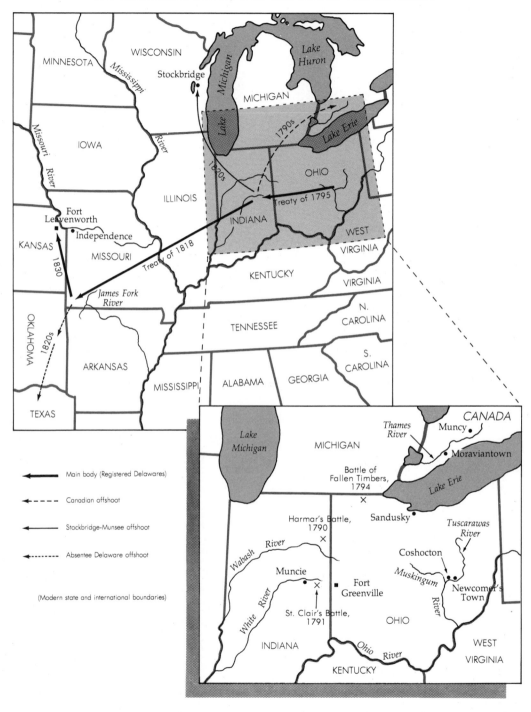

MINNESOTA

WISCONSIN

Stockbridge

Mississippi

IOWA

River

ILLINOIS

Missouri River

Fort Leavenworth

Independence

KANSAS

MISSOURI

1790s

1820s

MICHIGAN

Lake Michigan

Lake Huron

Lake Erie

OHIO

INDIANA

Treaty of 1795

WEST VIRGINIA

Treaty of 1818

1830

James Fork River

OKLAHOMA

1820s

ARKANSAS

MISSISSIPPI

TEXAS

KENTUCKY

VIRGINIA

TENNESSEE

N. CAROLINA

S. CAROLINA

ALABAMA

GEORGIA

Main body (Registered Delawares)

Canadian offshoot

Stockbridge-Munsee offshoot

Absentee Delaware offshoot

(Modern state and international boundaries)

Lake Michigan

MICHIGAN

Thames River

Muncy

CANADA

Moraviantown

Battle of Fallen Timbers, 1794

×

Sandusky

Lake Erie

Harmar's Battle, 1790

×

Tuscarawas River

Coshocton

Wabash River

Muscingum River

Newcomer's Town

White River

Muncie

×

Fort Greenville

St. Clair's Battle, 1791

OHIO

INDIANA

Ohio River

KENTUCKY

WEST VIRGINIA

toll. Their towns had been destroyed, their fields burned, and their possessions plundered. The English withdrawal from Ohio had put an end to diplomatic gifts from contending powers competing for Delaware support. The end of the colonial wars had also put Delaware warriors out of work. Finally, Delaware fur-trappers and traders now faced unemployment as low demand, due to changing fashions in Europe, caused the fur market to collapse.

The Delawares were despondent. The Americans were invariably victorious in war. What they did not take in war, they claimed at the conference table. Without hope for the future, many Delawares turned to alcohol. Some, more hopeful, turned once again to religion.

Again, prophets arose to guide the people. One woman, a Munsee named Beate, called upon her people to revive their ancient traditions. In Indiana it was difficult to follow the old ways. In the early 1800s, the impoverished Delawares worked longer and harder than ever before but, nonetheless, they had little time and less money for ritual and ceremony. Beate advised her people to combine their religious celebrations into a single ceremony in October lasting 12 days.

Beate also knew how many of her people felt about whites, and the ceremony that she is credited with originating rejected everything associated with them. This feeling was dramatically expressed in the Xingwikaon, or

A view of the interior of the Delaware Indian Big House in Copan, Oklahoma. The central beam has a carving of a mesingw, the Delaware game spirit, on the upper half. The Big House was the site of Delaware ceremonies that stressed traditional practices and values.

"Big House," which served as the home of the new ceremony. Only natural materials were used in its construction: Iron nails, glass windows, and other materials associated with Europeans were not permitted.

The Delawares called their new observance the Big House Ceremony. The Big House itself symbolized the universe in a small place. Its four walls represented the four grandparents of the Lenape creation story. The floor was the earth. The roof represented the heavens. The central post, decorated with carvings of mesingw, was a vertical shaft connecting the earth with the upper and lower worlds. And the oval dance floor, where men and woman prayed, danced, and sang of their spirit visions, was the "Beautiful White Path" of stars that is now called the Milky Way, the high road traveled by spirits.

Christian missionaries and converts also came to Indiana, but few Delawares listened with any interest now. The Moravians in particular lost many followers and much of their influence during this time. The Gnadenhutten massacre had shown that pacificism did not work on the violent frontier. The increasingly isolated Moravian Delawares finally moved north with a group of Munsees during the 1790s, and both communities settled in what is today the Province of Ontario. The Canadians gave the Munsees a reserve about 50 miles north of Lake Erie on the banks of the Thames River, at a village called Muncy, near the present-day town of Thamesville, Ontario. Thirty miles downriver, the Moravian Delawares built their own settlements around what has since become known as the Moraviantown Reserve.

Most Delawares were determined not to share the fate of their Munsee and Moravian kinfolk. Many young Delawares rejected Moravian pacificism and prayer. They instead supported the efforts of the Shawnee prophet Tenskwatawa and his brother, the war chief Tecumseh, to rebuild the Indian confederacy during the early 1800s. These Shawnee brothers lived among the Delawares at this time, and were influenced by the Delawares' religious traditions. Tenskwatawa not only preached that Europeans were evil but also encouraged followers to persecute and kill as witches more moderate Indians who were suspected of advocating peaceful coexistence with the Americans.

Many young Delawares became devoted followers of Tenskwatawa. Eager to rid their villages of anyone friendly with Americans, they accused several of their tribespeople of witchcraft. Most of the accused had been converted by Moravian missionaries. Most were still devout Christians, and many had accepted white ways of dress and other outward signs of the mainstream life. In the spring of 1806, several of these suspected witches were tortured and burned to death by Tenskwatawa's followers at the Indiana town of Wapekommekoke. Among the victims was the old and respected chief Tetepachsit. Tetepachsit, long a friend of the Moravians and an opponent of the Shawnee brothers, was tortured to "admit" that the Moravians were witches. When he later recanted, he was burned to death by members of his own tribe. The murder deeply split the Delawares.

Most, including many who shared the Shawnee prophet's goals, were outraged by the killings. Head chief William Anderson of the Indiana Delawares opposed Tenskwatawa, as did the influential American traders

The Shawnee prophet Tenskwatawa, "the Open Door," painted in 1832 by James Otto Lewis. The Indian spiritual leader led militant resistance to U.S. expansion before the War of 1812.

John and William Connor. Working with the Great Council, they persuaded most Delawares to withdraw their support of the Shawnee brothers. The Delawares' strict neutrality helped ensure the ultimate defeat of Tecumseh's forces and his confederacy at the Battle of the Thames near Moraviantown on October 5, 1813.

Neutrality allowed the Indiana Delawares to concentrate on preserving their remaining lands and traditions. Eager to add to their dwindling num-

bers, they invited their scattered kinfolk to join them. Many Delawares answered the call. Delawares from the Brotherton reservation in New Jersey; Stockbridge-Munsee Indians from Massachusetts; Long Island and Esopus Indians from New York; and the last remaining Ohio Delawares all moved to Indiana during these years. This migration was largely complete by 1840.

Even these few hundred immigrants could not give the Delawares, who now numbered around 3,000 at the most, enough strength to resist the Americans. Soon tens of thousands of settlers poured into Indiana after the British were completely forced out of U.S. territory in the War of 1812. This settlers' invasion was supported by a new U.S. government policy known as removal. Formalized in the Indian Removal Act of 1830, it called for the relocation of all Indians east of the Mississippi River to an Indian territory to be established on the prairies of Missouri, Kansas, and Oklahoma, then known as the Great American Desert.

Once again marauding settlers attacked Delaware people and pillaged their cabins. Refusing to protect them, agents appointed by the U.S. government to oversee the Indians (as part of what would ultimately become the Bureau of Indian Affairs, or BIA) relentlessly pressed Anderson and the other Delaware chiefs to sell their land. Under the terms of several treaties, they exchanged their Indiana lands for territory to the west of supposedly equal value. The Americans promised to compensate the Delawares for all losses and to pay annuities—yearly payments of cash and distributions of goods—to help them make a start in their new homes.

Finally, at a large treaty meeting attended by several tribes in St. Marys, Ohio, on October 3, 1818, the Delawares gave up virtually all of their remaining lands in Indiana and Ohio. In return, they were promised lands west of the Mississippi, awarded perpetual annuities amounting to nearly $5,000 for the entire tribe, and given horses, wagons, and provisions for the journey. A number of important chiefs also secretly received individual annual payments for the rest of their life as a reward for agreeing to the treaty provisions.

Farther east, most of the remaining Delawares also prepared to leave their lands. Stockbridge-Munsees living among the Oneida Iroquois in New York, including many Munsees and nearly 100 Brotherton Delawares from New Jersey, had been invited by Chief Anderson to settle along the White River in Indiana. The first few Stockbridge-Munsees to arrive, however, found that the lands promised them had already been sold. After receiving payments under the terms of the 1818 treaty, they decided not to join those Delawares journeying to the western Plains. Instead, they moved north to the forests of Wisconsin.

A few other Delaware communities clung to their lands in New York, Pennsylvania, and Ohio. One group of 100

Delawares, led by Solomon Journeycake, clung to their lands in Sandusky, Ohio. Most, however, were soon forced west by other treaties. By 1840, virtually all organized Delaware communities had relocated to the west. Many Delawares living in Cattaraugus, New York, moved with their Seneca Iroquois neighbors to the Six Nations Reserve in Ontario, Canada. Most of the last New Jersey Indians moved with their Brotherton and Stockbridge-Munsee kinfolk to Wisconsin. Other Munsees joined their brethren in Muncy, Ontario, or moved to Kansas.

American officials first resettled the main body of the Delawares alongside

An 1830 painting of an East Texas Delaware Indian. The Delawares were encouraged by Mexico to settle in Texas to act as a barrier to U.S. expansion.

the Shawnees and other displaced eastern tribes in southwestern Missouri during the early 1820s. The journey west was a hard one. Many, especially children and elders, died along the way. Still led by Anderson, the Delawares built their towns along the James Fork River. Their new towns were located on low-lying and swampy lands subject to frequent flooding. To make matters worse, they were on land claimed by the Osages. Fighting soon broke out as Delaware and Osage hunters competed for game.

The Delawares were unhappy in Missouri. Unable to make a living there, hunters had to travel farther north and west on horseback to find buffalo. These Delawares increasingly adopted the more nomadic customs and manners of many of the Plains Indian tribes they met while hunting on the western prairies.

Not all Indiana Delawares settled on the James Fork. Several hundred joined earlier immigrants elsewhere in Missouri and in Arkansas. Many of these "Absentee" Delawares (so called because they "absented" themselves from the main body) were invited by the Mexicans to settle in eastern Texas after Mexico won its independence from Spain in 1821. (The Mexican government hoped the Indian tribes would effectively constitute a shield against U.S. expansionism.) There the Delawares allied themselves with Cherokees, Choctaws, Creeks, and other tribes that had been forced to leave their southeastern homelands by the United States.

The Texas Delawares initially lived on good terms with their Mexican and Indian neighbors. White settlers, however, once again flooded into the region. Indian relations with these neighbors deteriorated following the successful Texan revolt against Mexico in 1836. Texas declared itself an independent republic in that year, and allowed itself to be annexed by the United States in 1845. Many Delawares, including the noted scout Black Beaver, helped the Americans during the two-year Mexican War that followed in 1846. Many continued thereafter to raid Mexican towns for horses or fought with Osages and Pawnees on the Great Plains. As a reward for their services, several Delawares were given small plots of land, and a reservation for the Delaware people was established on the Brazos River, Texas, in 1853. Indians were not, however, welcome in the new state. The Texas legislature, calling for the expulsion of all Indians, ordered the Absentee Delawares to abandon their Brazos lands in 1859. Most then moved north to live among the Wichita Indians in Indian Territory, now the state of Oklahoma.

Meanwhile, life in southwestern Missouri became increasingly unpleasant for the main body of Delawares. Poverty, epidemics, famine, conflict with neighboring tribes, and raids from local settlers again plagued their towns. Once again, American agents pressed them to sell their lands and move on. This time the Delawares moved willingly. In 1830 most settled on a new

Delaware Indian leader, guide, and tracker
Black Beaver, photographed about 1869.

low hunters to travel in comparative safety to buffalo-hunting grounds in Colorado and Nebraska.

Many Delawares from Wisconsin, Ontario, and elsewhere soon joined the main body near Fort Leavenworth. Shortly after 1830, the Kansas Delaware population swelled to more than 1,500. Nearby, on reservations of their own, lived the Shawnees and other old friends. Government agents paid for new log cabins, frame houses, barns, mills, and schools. Resigned to life among the Americans, most Delawares resolved to learn as much as they could about them. They invited Baptist and Presbyterian preachers to build missions and teach American customs and manners. Government agents hired teachers and blacksmiths to work on the reservation. Annuity payments in cash, and distributions of tools, seed, and livestock helped ease the Delawares' adjustment to their new homes. The Kansas Delawares soon became noted as breeders of excellent horses, cattle, sheep, and hogs.

In the Great Plains, Delawares became known as skilled hunters, guides, and trackers. Black Beaver, James Secondine, and John C. Connor guided explorers such as John C. Frémont and naturalists such as James Audubon on their expeditions. Adventurous Delawares traveled across the continent. Many trapped beavers in the Rocky Mountains.

It was not long, however, before the Kansas Delawares again found themselves in the path of American expan-

reservation of nearly 2 million acres on the Missouri River at Fort Leavenworth, in what would become the state of Kansas. The eastern portion consisted of rich farmlands and pastures. Much of the rest, however, was a dry, treeless strip of land only 10 miles wide, extending 200 miles west onto the Plains. This "Delaware Strip" did, however, alsion. At first, settlers heading to Oregon and New Mexico merely wanted to pass through the Kansas reservation. More settlers, however, soon followed, setting up their own communities along the trails. Tensions increased as these local whites gave Delawares liquor, sold them shoddy goods, and stole their horses.

American agents appeared once again as the Kansas settlers demanded the Delawares' removal. Bending to these pressures, the Delawares sold their reservation piece by piece in a series of treaties between 1854 and 1866. During this time, pro- and antislavery forces made the region a battleground. The Delawares attempted to remain neutral, but this became impossible when the Civil War finally broke out in 1861. Kansas achieved statehood that year, and most Delawares fought for the Union during the struggle, hoping to halt further loss of their lands by earning American goodwill. Support of the Union, however, did not halt the government's efforts to acquire Delaware lands. Although Delawares had sacrificed much for the Union, the government forced them to sell the last of their Kansas reservation in 1866, only one year after the end of the Civil War. Watching helplessly as government agents cooperated with the railroads to take their lands, the Delawares sold the last of their reservation for $2.50 an acre and began to move south, to Indian Territory. ▲

Enoch, an Absentee Delaware, photographed about 1870.

TOWARD
THE
TWENTIETH
CENTURY

The 1,000 Delawares who moved to Indian Territory immediately after the sale of their Kansas reservation in 1866 settled among the Cherokees. The move from Kansas was not easy. Once again, cabins, farms, fields, and friends had to be left behind. Once again, mills, schools, stores, churches, and the graves of loved ones had to be abandoned. Once again, exposed to both extremely hot and cold weather, some young and old sickened and died on the way. And once again, new problems confronted them at the end of the trail.

In the 1850s, every man, woman, and child on the Kansas reservation had been granted private ownership of 80 acres. They had continued to own the rest of the reservation as a tribe. Profits from the sale of these commonly owned lands to settlers, other Indians, and the railroad companies were held in trust for the Delawares by government agents. Using these tribal funds, each of the Kansas Delawares now pur-

chased 160 acres of Cherokee property for a dollar an acre—a total of 160,000 acres of land in the Cherokee Nation, along the Caney River valley in what is today northeastern Oklahoma.

The Delawares soon discovered that their Cherokee hosts were not especially friendly or generous. Living in Confederate-dominated country, the Cherokees, like most of the Oklahoma tribes, had fought on the rebel side during the just-ended Civil War. More than 80 percent of all Kansas Delaware men, on the other hand, had served as Union volunteers. Neither tribe had wanted to fight, but each had done so to get the protection of their allies. The antagonisms of the war still lingered.

The Cherokees pressed hard terms upon the Delawares. Although the asking price for their lands was low, they also demanded that all Delawares moving among them become Cherokee citizens. If the Delawares did so, they would be giving up their independence to be governed by the Cherokees.

The Delawares whose names appeared on the list of those eligible to receive money from the sale of Kansas reservation lands were known as "Registered" Delawares. They were welcomed by the Cherokees as a much-needed addition to their depleted tribal ranks. Cherokee officials extended their

Delaware leader John C. Connor, painted by Friedrich Petri in the 1850s. Connor was the son of William Connor, a trader from Indiana, and Mekinges, the daughter of a Delaware chief. He served as a guide and tracker for the U.S. cavalry.

nation's citizenship to Registered Delawares and promised to act in their best interests. Cherokee and Delaware ideas of best interest, however, did not coincide exactly.

The Cherokees demanded that the Registered Delawares share their tribal funds with them. Yet the Cherokees refused to share the contents of their own national treasury in return. Relations worsened when Cherokees tried to tell Delawares where to locate their homesteads along the Caney River. Resenting these and other actions, the Delawares resisted Cherokee authority, leading to endless litigation in tribal courts controlled by Cherokees. The Delawares, unable to obtain justice in these courts, frequently turned to federal authorities for protection and assistance.

One group of Kansas Delawares, Christian Munsees who had moved from Wisconsin during the 1830s, refused to relocate to Indian Territory. Marrying into non-Indian families a few miles south of Fort Leavenworth in Franklin County, they renounced their Indian status, became American citizens, bought farms as private owners, and blended into American society. Still other Delawares moved elsewhere. The followers of John C. Connor, the son of Chief Anderson's daughter Mekinges and Indiana trader William Connor, moved instead to the Peoria Indian Reservation in Neosho, Kansas. Many of these people gave up their tribal status in 1873 and took up private title to their lands there.

Most Kansas Delawares, however, ultimately moved to Indian Territory, intended at that time as a final tribal homeland for all Indians. Also resettling in Indian Territory were the Absentee Delawares who had moved to Texas in the 1820s. After that state forced virtually all Indians to leave in 1859, many moved north into Indian Territory. These Delawares, along with many other tribes, had settled at the Wichita Agency. They were forced to leave their houses and many of their possessions behind. Much of their livestock was lost on the trail. More than a few people died.

The Absentee Delawares quickly built new log houses at the Wichita Agency. Many improvements, however, had to wait until the end of the Civil War. The war divided Indians at the agency. Like the Delawares in Kansas, most Absentee Delawares supported the Union. A few of the former Texas Indians at Wichita, however, fought for the Confederacy, seeing the war as an opportunity to get their homes back by showing loyalty to the Confederate cause.

The Absentee Delawares, and most other Wichita Agency Indians, fled north to Kansas in 1861. During the war, Black Beaver and other Absentee Delawares performed important services as Union scouts and soldiers. After the war ended, most did not immediately return to their Indian Territory homes, as many of their houses had been destroyed in the fighting, and local feeling ran against those who had fought for the Union. By 1867, however, most had returned, settling this time near Anadarko.

In 1874, the Absentee Delawares placed themselves under the jurisdiction of the Caddo Indians. One year later, it was reported that 61 Delawares lived at the Caddo agency, and that another 30 or so lived nearby on the Kiowa and Comanche reservations. This affiliation with the Caddoes was a generally harmonious one for the Absentees.

At Anadarko, the Absentee Delawares lived close to the Great Plains, working as trackers, scouts, and guides. On one occasion, the Delaware chief Jack Harry saved a band of Comanches from destruction by negotiating their surrender after he had guided a murderously inclined troop of cavalry to their camp. As the years passed, many of these Delawares came to live among and marry members of the Plains Indian tribes. These neighbors gradually adopted many aspects of their culture, and the Delawares in turn adopted some of theirs. Thus they would become the first Delawares to adopt the peyote religion as Comanches carried it north from Mexico during the 1880s.

Peyotism, also known as the Native American Church, combined elements of the traditional Indian religious beliefs and practices of various tribes with aspects of Christianity. Its central sacrament involved the chewing of a hallucinogenic, but nonaddictive, substance from the peyote cactus. Taken during religious services, peyote pro-

duced vivid visions believed to clear worshipers' thoughts and bring them closer to the spirits.

One of the most influential preachers of Peyotism was a man of mixed Delaware and Caddo ancestry named John Wilson. Wilson's version of the religion, known as the Big Moon rite (after the large, moon-shaped altar used in the ceremony), combined such traditional Indian elements as the vision quest, the tipi, the pipe, and the prayer rattles and fans with Christian elements such as belief in Jesus, the Holy Sacrament, and the cross. Wilson first brought Peyotism to the Absentee Delawares in western Indian Territory in the 1880s, and it was later brought to eastern Oklahoma.

Not all Delaware communities accepted Peyotism. Most Canadian Delawares, for example, showed limited interest in the Native American Church. Most Munsees in Kansas also refused to accept the religion and generally adopted mainstream Christianity, as did the Stockbridge-Munsees of Wisconsin.

Most Stockbridge-Munsees struggled to live in peace with their non-Indian Wisconsin neighbors. After moving several times, they finally settled on densely wooded lands directly below the Menominee reservation. During the 1840s, members of the Stockbridge-Munsee Citizens Party, which favored accepting American citizenship, had divided their part of the 23,000 acre reservation into privately owned parcels. (The remaining acres continued to be held by the community.) Wisconsin achieved statehood in 1848, and the following decade, in 1856, the tribe itself adopted a constitution based upon that of the U.S. government.

The people of the Stockbridge-Munsee community took pride in their successful adjustment to mainstream culture. Yet they also carefully pre-

served their Indian traditions of maintaining close family ties and being generous and cooperative with one another. Unlike their non-Indian neighbors, who felled entire forests for quick profit, the Stockbridge-Munsees cared for their land by selectively harvesting the same amount of timber every year. It would be many decades before most Americans accepted the wisdom of this type of forestry.

Stockbridge-Munsee men worked in the logging industry and found employment in nearby towns and cities. As time went on, most of these families joined Christian churches. Those who refused to do so often moved to more traditional communities in Indian Territory.

The Canadian Munsees generally followed the same path as their Stockbridge-Munsee kinfolk. Most Moraviantown Delawares had maintained their Christian beliefs after coming to Ontario in 1792. Working as farmers, they lived quietly alongside their non-Indian neighbors. Many Delawares and Munsees living in Muncy, Ontario, or among the Iroquois at the Six Nations Reserve, also, adopted many non-Indian ways during the 19th century. Most Canadian Delawares became members of the Anglican or Methodist churches, and in 1852 the last Big House in Canada was torn down. Many of the people found work in factories and offices as mechanization made small-scale farming less profitable.

Whether in Canada, Wisconsin, Kansas, or Indian Territory, by the

This pictograph, carved into a boulder in the New York Botanical Garden, represents a turtle, widely believed to be a Delaware clan totem.

1860s Delawares lived in a culture that had undergone profound changes since Europeans had first come among them 300 years earlier. They had abandoned many of their ancient ways, and their numbers had dwindled disastrously— from as many as 24,000 people in 1600 to a total of 2,000 in 1866. A few hundred more were scattered in remote settlements among New Jersey to the western Canadian provinces of Alberta and British Columbia.

Scattered as they were, it was difficult for Delawares to find spouses among their own people. They increasingly married members of other tribes.

No matter where they moved, however, they maintained their traditional kinship system of the three clans—Turkey, Turtle, and Wolf. These clans lost their matrilineal emphasis, however, as exile forced women to give up their traditional clan lands and properties. Increasingly, both men and women came to own land and share labor, and increasing numbers of Delawares would trace descent from the father's side as their greater participation in the mainstream economy emphasized male job holding at the expense of women's work in the home.

Delawares across the continent took more than kinship customs from the mainstream culture during the 19th century. Many adopted the dominant culture's dress, manners, and attitudes. Many learned to speak, read, and write English. Hundreds were educated in mission schools. A number, including the influential Stockbridge-Munsee clan leader (and Christian preacher) John W. Quinney, received college educations in schools such as Dartmouth. Educated Delawares were often more literate than their non-Indian neighbors.

As political, economic, and social changes transformed the Delawares' culture, their ideas about land ownership shifted from communal to private forms. No longer able to subsist as traders, warriors, hunters, or basket makers, most turned to farming, ranching, or lumbering. These industries required enormous investments of time and money. Needing to accumulate capital, most Delawares could no longer afford to be as sharing or as generous as their ancestors had been.

Delaware traditions of tolerance and flexibility had helped them survive years of forced removals. But now the forces of social change placed great strains upon them. Progressives accepting mainstream ways argued with conservatives holding fast to tradition. Everywhere, Christians vied with Indian traditionalists for the conscience of the people.

Stockbridge-Munsee leader and Christian preacher John W. Quinney, painted by George Catlin in 1836.

The Registered Delawares, who had settled among the Cherokees in Indian Territory in 1866, continued to struggle for recognition by authorities of the Cherokee Nation. After years of litigation in tribal courts, Registered Delawares, led by their last traditional chief, Charles Journeycake, at last appealed to the federal courts. There they finally won full rights as Cherokee citizens in 1890. This victory gave the Delawares equitable shares of Cherokee money and equal justice, but it heralded the end of their own nation. Because they had accepted Cherokee citizenship, the Registered Delawares were dissolved as a distinct tribe. This dissolution would soon be calamitous for the Delawares, owing to the repercussions of the General Allotment Act.

The General Allotment Act, also called the Dawes Act after its author, Senator Henry L. Dawes, was one of the most devastating implements of U.S. assimilation policies. Written into law in 1887 (though its full effects would not be felt by the Registered Delawares until around 1904), it required the division of tribally held reservation lands into small, privately owned plots. Although terms varied from tribe to tribe, heads of households were generally given, or allotted, 160 acres each. The government Indian agents, often ignoring traditional clan affiliations or family groupings, determined who would be considered the head of a household. It was considered desirable to teach the Indians the benefits of private land ownership and thereby draw

An advertisement for the sale of Indian Territory land to non-Indians in 1879. To lure purchasers, it declares, "Indians are rejoicing to have the whites settle up this country."

them into wider society. Thus the law weakened tribal ties by ending communal ownership of land; it also provided more land for homesteaders, as the land remaining after each household had received its parcel was considered surplus and sold off to non-Indians. The proceeds from the sale of this "excess" land to settlers were held for, and usually distributed among, the Indians, who were now private landowners themselves.

Like the communally owned land of earlier days, each Indian's privately owned land was exempt from state and local laws and taxes so long as it remained in Indian ownership. But those Indians who accepted the idea of private property were granted U.S. citizenship—and with it, the burden of taxation. And although the Allotment Act prohibited them from selling their land for a specified number of years, most land could eventually be sold. The Indians, soon desperate for money to survive, often ended up selling their land for far less than its fair value.

This chain of events, engendered by the Dawes Act, had ravaged other tribes, and it would soon do the same to the Delawares. Having accepted citizenship in the Cherokee Nation in 1890, the Registered Delawares were powerless to keep their Cherokee hosts from accepting allotment in 1902. This action dissolved the Cherokee Nation, abolished its reservation, and forced acceptance of U.S. citizenship on all its former members—including the Registered Delawares. Following complex formulations and much political intrigue, each of the 890 Registered Delawares was now allotted an average of 60 acres. Many of these allotments were far from the Delaware communities, which were centered in Washington County. The remainder of the 157,600 acres claimed by the Delawares was sold off to non-Indians.

Suddenly, the Delawares found that they had lost not only their nation, but their status as Indians as well. Within months of the dissolution of the Cherokee Nation, all Delaware lands along the Caney River were divided up into sections and allotted among individual Delawares. Those lands remaining after each Delaware had received an allotment were thrown open to non-Indians, and the resulting income was divided among the tribal members. Loss of their national status brought poverty once again to Delaware families. Lump-sum payments of annuities and other moneys were soon spent. A number of their allotments were confiscated for nonpayment of taxes after Oklahoma became a state in 1907. Within a few years, many Delawares were landless, unemployed, and adrift in a society in which whites were treated better than everybody else.

Delawares refused to give in to poverty and demoralization, and fought back in federal court. Richard C. Adams, a Delaware Christian preacher and community leader, led an effort to defend their people's rights and get compensation for their losses. On April 12, 1904, Congress awarded $150,000 to satisfy all outstanding claims of Delawares living in the former Cherokee Nation. But because Adams and his associates were unable to convince Congress to restore Delaware tribal status, lost lands could not be recovered. Many Delaware families sank deeper into debt and despair. For them, the start of a new century meant little. ▲

Delaware leaders take part in a reburial ceremony for human remains found on New York's Ellis Island. The reburial was performed on June 28, 1987, with the cooperation of the National Park Service.

INTO
THE FUTURE

In his landmark 1907 study of American Indian groups, Smithsonian Institution anthropologist James A. Mooney estimated that nearly 1,900 Delawares lived in predominantly Indian communities in Oklahoma, Kansas, Wisconsin, and Ontario. Of these, wrote Mooney, 870 had been incorporated into the Cherokee Nation in Indian Territory; 95 were living on the Wichita Agency; an estimated 260 Stockbridge-Munsees lived in Wisconsin; perhaps 45 more Munsees dwelt with the Chippewas in Kansas; 347 Moravian Delawares lived along the Thames River in Ontario, with 122 Munsees living nearby; and 150 Delawares lived with the Six Nations on the Grand River in Ontario.

Several hundred more Delawares lived in or near mostly non-Indian towns scattered throughout America and Canada, from the Atlantic Coast to the Rocky Mountains. Mooney's figures showed, in effect, that during the last half of the 19th century the Delawares had not experienced the sharp drop in population that afflicted most tribes forced to give up their lands and traditional ways of life. It seemed that hard-earned wisdom from their three centuries of experience with Old World diseases and intruders had helped the Delawares cope with the settlers flooding across the western prairies.

The new influx of settlers provided opportunities to many Delawares. Wage labor became important; many Delaware men found employment as farmhands, ranch hands, and cowboys, and Delaware women worked as dressmakers, house servants, and nursemaids. Delawares also found work as laborers in the towns and cities that sprang up in or near their own communities. Delaware workers now came to depend, like their non-Indian neighbors, upon supplies obtained in local stores or through mail-order catalogs, buying seeds, flour, sugar, tea, tools, and other items. Although they continued to decorate their clothing, tools, and weapons with traditional Indian designs, Delawares now purchased most of these objects. Increasingly, people wore broad-brimmed felt hats and ready-made suits and other garments as the animals needed to make hide- and fur-based clothing disappeared as a result of overhunting.

With the opportunities presented by settlements came difficulties. At first, settlers and shopkeepers readily hired Delawares and sought their patronage. Newer settlers, however, resented this competition and quickly took all but the most demeaning jobs. Delawares seeking credit from local stores soon found themselves unwelcome.

Differing ideas about proper land use also caused friction between Delawares and settlers. The Delawares continued to share their lands with their kinfolk, leaving most land open and fencing only small garden plots. Cattle and game animals ranged freely across the unfenced tribal lands. New settlers, anxious over the safety of their property, crops, and livestock, fenced their pastures and fields. They also shot or poisoned wild animals—not only those that might prey upon their herds, but harmless animals that might lure predators as well. As a result, most game animals the Delawares needed for food were exterminated or scared away within a few years.

Unable to hunt or earn enough to feed and clothe their families, many Delawares became increasingly unable to resist Canadian and American governmental efforts to control their life. Elders found it increasingly difficult to pass on their ancient ways, and many customs disappeared as educators, missionaries, and government agents actively discouraged their practice. Ancient tribal governments led by he-reditary chiefs and councillors also disappeared as the Canadian and American authorities abolished tribes and imposed the laws of their own governments.

Among these laws were ones requiring Indian children to attend government-run schools. Many of these schools were thousands of miles away from their intended students, so that children were forced to become boarders, separated from their parents and native environment for long stretches of time. At these schools, impressionable young Delawares were discouraged from wearing traditional clothing, practicing old customs, and speaking their native languages. They were instead encouraged to become members of the mainstream society. In their eagerness to make these children like themselves, many teachers ignored or even ridiculed the teachings of Delaware elders.

The entry of young Delawares into the cultural mainstream meant the extinction of many ancient practices. Several Delaware languages disappeared in the early 1900s as the last speakers of Mahican and a number of Munsee and Unami dialects grew old and died without transmitting their knowledge to the young. The Big House Ceremony gradually lost popularity as its last visionaries grew old and died. Big House ritualists had more and more difficulty assembling enough people to observe the ceremony properly, and the increasing scarcity of game made it difficult to find the deer essential for feasts

Young Delaware women photographed in Oklahoma about 1910. The woman on the far left wears the insignia of the Carlisle Indian School on her sweater.

and sacrifices. The last complete Big House Ceremony was held in 1924. Although shortened versions were held during World War II for the welfare of Delaware servicemen, the Big House is now only a distant memory among Delaware elders.

Many former Big House celebrants, however, came to attend traditional ceremonies held by the Shawnees and their other Indian neighbors. The Peyotism that had spread among the tribes of the Great Plains in the late 1880s also attracted a number of Dela-

ware adherents in the first decade of the new century.

But, like the Big House, Peyotism lost much of its popularity as most Delawares increasingly adopted the Christian beliefs prevalent among their American and Canadian neighbors. Today, however, numerous Delawares maintain an affiliation with the Native American Church. As a people, the Delawares continue to be deeply spiritual. Active Protestant communities exist in every Delaware community, and most Delaware individuals strive to apply

Christian principles in their everyday lives.

Christian missionaries were among the many representatives of mainstream society who exposed young Delawares to the possibilities of life in the wider world. Inspired by these emissaries, many young Delawares looked forward to leaving their small, tightly regulated communities. Others, such as John W. Quinney in Wisconsin and Richard Adams in Oklahoma, became Christian ministers themselves. Still others, however, watched sadly as their elders died without passing on all their knowledge of the ancient ways.

Traditionalists such as Charley Elkhair and Jonathan "Charley" Weber, for example, continued the struggle to convey Delaware customs to future generations. They taught the younger Delawares and also cooperated with anthropologists—scholars trained in the study of human cultures—to see that the old ways did not die. In the early 1900s the scholarly anthropological community recognized that the government's assimilation policies were

The Delaware xingwikaon, *or Big House, in Copan, Oklahoma, photographed about 1916. The last complete Big House ceremony was held in Copan in 1924.*

threatening many Indian cultures. Eager to preserve a record of them, universities and museums employed anthropologists to seek out knowledgeable elders and record their traditions. The works of Frank Speck and Mark Raymond Harrington, listed in this book's bibliography, remain a vital source of information on traditional Delaware religion and society.

Allotment of tribal land to individual Delawares and the sale of the remainder was completed by 1910. In the following decade, an oil boom swept Oklahoma, but though oil was found on some Delawares' lands, tribal loss of mineral rights kept most from benefiting from the discovery.

Recognizing the disastrous effects of allotment, Congress in 1924 granted U.S. citizenship to all resident Indians whether they accepted the benefits of private property or not. Similar laws were passed in Canada. Citizenship promised Indians participation in government and legal protection in the courts. It also, however, threatened their hard-earned treaty guarantees of special protection, still needed by a people not yet fully accepted as equals in American society.

Jobs were always hard for the ostracized Delawares to find and became even more elusive during the Great Depression of the 1930s, which affected both the U.S. and Canada. As a result of severe drought and harsh windstorms that blew away the topsoil, Oklahoma in particular became known as the Dust Bowl, an arid near-desert

impossible to farm successfully. Needing work to support their parents and families, many young Delawares left their homes for towns and cities, relocating to Tulsa, St. Louis, Chicago, New York, and Los Angeles. Many soon lost touch with their old identities and customs.

All these changes transformed Delaware culture to some degree. Loss of tribal lands and status, however, had the greatest continuing impact. Although Canadian Delawares were permitted by their government to keep their reserves, much of the land on them was nonetheless sold off to non-Indians.

In the United States, the election of Franklin D. Roosevelt to the presidency in 1932 brought about major changes in governmental Indian policy. Alarmed by the devastation caused by allotment, and recognizing that Indians had been especially hard hit by the continuing depression, the Roosevelt administration oversaw the enactment of new legislation, most notably the Indian Reorganization Act (IRA) of 1934, designed to protect extant tribal governments. The IRA set forth a procedure by which it would recognize and support the tribal status of those Indian communities that voted to adopt constitutions providing for a representative government. The Stockbridge-Munsees, however, were the only American Delawares to achieve IRA recognition. After rewriting their earlier tribal constitution, the Stockbridge-Munsees were officially recognized as an Indian tribe on May 21, 1938. The funds they subsequently received from the federal government as a result of this recognition process were used to purchase more than 15,000 acres for a new reservation within the boundaries of their earlier, now defunct Wisconsin reservation.

Other Delaware communities continued to press claims against the U.S. and Canadian governments for redress of historical injustices. Convinced of their rightness by the court judgement and award of 1904, Delaware leaders continually spoke of unfair treatment and of promises made, then broken.

The Indian Claims Commission (ICC) was established in 1946, giving Delawares another chance to press these claims. It was created as American sentiment was once again swinging toward the assimilation of Indians into the mainstream and used its power to that end. The ICC established a temporary federal court empowered to hear and rule on Indian damage claims against the U.S. government. Successful claimants were granted cash settlements based upon the value of their lost land at the time of the original treaty or purchase. The goal of the ICC was simple: to satisfy all outstanding Indian claims so that all remaining federal responsibilities to the tribes could be terminated. It was expected that once claims were resolved, Indians as individuals would be assimilated into the cultural mainstream. This policy was known as termination.

Several communities of Delawares hired attorneys to file petitions with the ICC over lands taken from them unfairly or purchased at inadequate prices through old treaties and land sales. Many of these suits were successful. The Stockbridge-Munsees, for example, shared in a $1.3 million settlement with their neighbors, the Wisconsin Oneidas and other emigrant New York Indian tribes.

Lawyers representing 6,446 descendants of the main body of Delawares in Oklahoma and 1,480 members of the Western Oklahoma Tribe of Delawares also filed a series of suits seeking reparations. Arguing that the Stockbridge-Munsees had become a separate tribe, Oklahoma Delaware lawyers excluded that group from any share in their own claims. These suits eventually won more than $15 million in settlements—more than $2,000 per individual claimant.

The Absentee Delawares had few problems in distributing their share of this claim money to their people. They used part of it to establish a tribal fund that continues to support tribal health, housing, and administrative programs.

Several disputes, still unresolved as of the late 1980s, prevented the distribution of the share belonging to the Registered Delawares in eastern Oklahoma, however. The Cherokees, their former hosts, have insisted that these Delawares share the award with them. Many of the Registered Delawares also disagree among themselves about who

An Oklahoma Delaware man using a traditional fire-drill to start a fire, photographed by Mark R. Harrington in 1909. The drill was used in ceremonies to light a "pure" fire, or one created without the use of European-made matches.

should be eligible to receive the money, and argue about the method of its distribution. Some call for payments to individuals. Others ask that a certain amount be held in common to set up a tribal fund. These disputes reflect deep divisions within the community, and

the funds will remain under federal control until a resolution is reached.

Indian policies initiated during the civil rights era of the 1960s put an end to most governmental assimilation policies. New measures, associated with President Lyndon Johnson's War on Poverty, were enacted to support Indian communities and enhance the quality of their life. Indians shared in a range of programs meant to improve housing, health, education, and work opportunities for minority groups. As part of this, money, resources, and training were provided to U.S. Delaware communities.

The 1960s also marked a surge in ethnic consciousness and the rise of minority power. Delawares both benefited and suffered from increased visibility in the media created by the "Red Power" demonstrations of Indian activists and their supporters in the 1970s. Events staged by these demonstrators—such as the 1972 Trail of Broken Treaties caravan and subsequent sit-in at the Bureau of Indian Affairs in Washington, D.C., and the American Indian Movement's 1973 occupation of Wounded Knee, South Dakota—helped heighten public awareness of Indian problems. But they also created a backlash among some groups unfavorably disposed toward Indians.

The status of Indian affairs in Canada remains uncertain as of the late 1980s. The consequences of revisions to the Indian Act, brought on by the recent restoration of the Canadian Constitu-

Delaware Indian elder Nora Thompson Dean, photographed shortly before her death in 1984. She worked to keep traditions and language alive for present-day members of the Delaware tribe.

ditional identities even as they participate in American and Canadian society. Approximately 13,000 people are listed on various Delaware tribal rolls recognized by the U.S. and Canadian governments. Thousands more claim Delaware ancestry, though fewer than 20 people now speak the surviving Delaware language with any fluency. Delawares work on farms and in cities, holding jobs in industry, business, agriculture, and the professions. Delawares have served with distinction in the U.S. and Canadian military, and many have found positions in education and government. Tribal enterprises, such as gift shops, have been established in many Delaware communities and are managed by Indians.

Federally recognized tribal governments continue to operate on the Canadian Delaware reserves and the Stockbridge-Munsee Reservation in Wisconsin. Young Delawares have shown growing interest in their traditions in recent years, and elders continue to pass on the old ways to new generations.

One such elder was Nora Thompson Dean, also known as Touching Leaves Woman. Born into a tradition-minded Delaware family of eastern Oklahoma, Dean spoke Unami and became over the years a virtual repository of tribal learning. She operated a store featuring Indian crafts for her livelihood and was also recognized as a storyteller and one of the few elders qualified to act as a name-giver—one who assigns

tion, are not yet known. It remains an enduring irony of history, however, that both the Moravian Delawares, who supported the Americans, and the Munsees, who hated the U.S. government, have found themselves in permanent exile in Canada.

Today, the scattered Delaware communities struggle to preserve their tra-

traditional names to Delaware infants. During her lifetime, the governors of Oklahoma, Pennsylvania, and Delaware honored her as a gracious and patient teacher of tribal ways to scholars and children alike. Even her death—in Bartlesville, Oklahoma, on November 29, 1984, when she was in her eighties—became an occasion for the reunion of Delawares from across the country and the renewal of tribal attachments. ▲

BIBLIOGRAPHY

Goddard, R. H. Ives III. "Delaware." In *Handbook of North American Indians*. Vol. 15, *Northeast,* edited by R. H. Ives Goddard III, 213–39. Washington, DC: Smithsonian Institution, 1978.

Hale, Duane Kendall. *Peacemakers on the Frontier: A History of the Delaware Tribe of Western Oklahoma.* Anadarko, OK: Delaware Tribe of Western Oklahoma Press, 1987.

Harrington, Mark Raymond. *The Indians of New Jersey: Dickon Among the Lenape.* New Brunswick, NJ: Rutgers University Press, 1963.

———. "Religion and Ceremonies of the Lenape." Vol. 19, *Indian Notes and Monographs.* New York: Museum of the American Indian, Heye Foundation, 1921.

Kraft, Herbert C. *The Lenape: Archaeology, History, and Ethnography.* Newark: New Jersey Historical Society, 1986.

Myers, Albert Cook, ed. *William Penn: His Own Account of the Lenni Lenape or Delaware Indians.* Wallingford, PA: Middle Atlantic Press, 1970.

Richter, Conrad. *The Light in the Forest.* New York: Knopf, 1953.

Speck, Frank. "A Study of the Delaware Big House Ceremony." Vol. 2, *Publications of the Pennsylvania Historical Commission.* Harrisburg: Historical and Museum Commission, 1931.

Tantaquidgeon, Gladys. *Folk Medicine of the Delaware and Related Algonkian Indians.* Harrisburg: Pennsylvania Historical and Museum Commission, 1972.

Wallace, Anthony F. C. *King of the Delawares: Teedyuscung, 1700–1763.* Philadelphia: University of Pennsylvania Press, 1949.

Wallace, Paul A. W. *Indians in Pennsylvania.* Rev. ed. Harrisburg: Pennsylvania Historical and Museum Commission, 1981.

Weslager, C. A. *The Delaware Indians: A History.* New Brunswick, NJ: Rutgers University Press, 1972.

———. *The Delawares: A Critical Bibliography.* Bloomington: Indiana University Press, 1978.

THE LENAPES AT A GLANCE

TRIBE   *Lenapes (now known as Delawares and Munsees)*

CULTURE AREA   *Middle Atlantic*

TRADITIONAL GEOGRAPHY   *The middle Atlantic coast of the United States, between western Connecticut and northern Delaware at contact.*

LINGUISTIC FAMILY   *Algonquian*

CURRENT POPULATION   *approximately 13,000*

FIRST CONTACT   *Giovanni da Verrazano, Italian, 1524.*

MODERN STATUS   *Canada: two reserves at Moraviantown and Muncy, Ontario. Some Delawares live among Iroquois on the Six Nations Reserve in Ontario. United States: one reservation in Wisconsin, owned by the Stockbridge-Munsee branch of the Munsees; two communities of enrolled tribal members in Oklahoma; and unrecognized communities in several other states, including New Jersey, Pennsylvania, and Kansas.*

agent A person appointed by the Bureau of Indian Affairs to supervise U.S. government programs on a reservation and/or in a specific region. After 1908 the title *superintendent* replaced *agent*.

allotment U.S. policy applied nationwide through the General Allotment Act passed in 1887, aimed at breaking up tribally owned reservations by assigning individual farms and ranches to Indians. Allotment was intended as much to discourage traditional communal activities as to encourage private farming and assimilate Indians into mainstream American life.

breechcloth A strip of animal skin or cloth that is drawn between the legs and hung from a belt tied around the waist.

Bureau of Indian Affairs (BIA) A U.S. government agency now within the Department of the Interior. Originally intended to manage trade and other relations with Indians, the BIA now seeks to develop and implement programs that encourage Indians to manage their own affairs and to improve their educational opportunities and general social and economic well-being.

clan A multigenerational group having a shared identity, organization, and property, based on belief in their descent from common ancestor. Because clan members consider themselves closely related, marriage within a clan is strictly prohibited. The Lenapes were divided into three major clans: the Turkey, the Turtle, and the Wolf.

Covenant Chain The system of alliances between northeastern Indian tribes and British colonial officials, landowners, and traders in the 18th century. The British created the Covenant Chain to protect themselves from the French and their Indian allies.

culture The learned behavior of humans; nonbiological, socially taught activities; the way of life of a group of people.

Delawares One of the two divisions of the Lenape tribe. The Delawares spoke a dialect of the Lenape language known as Unami and inhabited the coastal plains of the Atlantic Ocean along what are now New York, New Jersey, and Delaware. The Indians changed their name to the Delaware in the 1750s to emphasize their independence as a nation when they were displaced from their homeland by European settlers.

dialect A regional variant of a particular language with unique elements of grammar, pronunciation, and vocabulary. The Lenape language still has two recognizable dialects—Unami (meaning "Downriver People") and Munsee (meaning "People from the Stony Country").

hominy A mush made from ground corn.

Indian Territory An area in the south central United States to which the U.S. government resettled Indians from other regions, especially the eastern states. In 1907, the territory became the state of Oklahoma.

Kishelemukong The Great Spirit or Creator of the Lenapes; literally, "He who creates us by his thoughts."

Lenapes An Indian tribe that traditionally lived on the northeastern coast of North America in what are now the states of New Jersey, New York, Delaware, and Pennsylvania. Today, the Lenapes are divided into the Delawares, primarily of the southwestern United States and southeastern Canada, and the Munsees of the northeastern United States and southeastern Canada. The word *lenape* literally means "people."

Lenapehoking The Delaware name for their ancestral homeland; literally, "the land of the people."

longhouse Dwelling, made of a cedar frame covered with bark and branches, used by many eastern North American tribes. These buildings were sometimes up to 100 feet long and could house 10 or 12 families.

manetuwak Lenape word for spirits.

matrilineal descent Rules for determining family or clan membership by tracking kinship through female ancestors.

Mesinghholikan Lenape participants in a dance to honor the "Mesingw" or game spirits, which were believed to control the animals that the Indians hunted.

mission A center founded by foreign advocates of a particular religion (especially Christianity) to try to convert the indigenous populations to their faith.

meteinuwak A Lenape doctor or medicine person.

Munsees One of the two divisions of the Lenape tribe. The Munsees (literally, "People from the Stony Country") traditionally inhabited the uplands of the lower Hudson and the upper Delaware rivers and spoke the Munsee dialect of the Lenape language. The Munsees now live primarily on two reserves in southeastern Canada but one branch, the Stockbridge-Munsee, lives on a reservation in southern Wisconsin.

Ohtas The Lenape Doll Being, a spirit believed to have powerful curing abilities. The Lenapes carved models of this spirit and performed yearly dances to honor it.

pictographs Images or symbols, often representing spirits or clan membership, that are carved on rock or bark.

polygyny The system of marriage in which a man may have more than one wife.

removal policy Federal policy, begun in 1830, calling for the sale of all Indian land in the eastern United States and the relocation of Indians indigenous to these areas to lands west of the Mississippi River.

reservation, reserve A tract of land retained by Indians for their own occupation and use. These areas are called *reservations* in the United States and *reserves* in Canada.

scalp lock A hairstyle worn by the members of many Indian tribes, including the Lenapes, in which the head is shaved except for a strip of hair down the center of the scalp.

Shouwunnock The Lenape word for Europeans, meaning "salty people."

sinew A dried, cured animal tendon used for making thread, bowstrings, and other useful items.

squatters People who occupy property without having legal title to it.

termination Federal policy to remove Indian tribes from government supervision and Indian lands from trust status, in effect from the late 1940s through the 1960s.

territory A defined region of the United States that is not, but may become, a state. The officials of a territory are appointed by the president, but territory residents elect their own legislature.

totem The emblem or symbol of a clan or family, usually the animal or plant that the family claims as its mythical ancestor.

treaty A contract negotiated between representatives of the U.S. government or another national government and one or more Indian tribes. Treaties may deal with the cessation of military action, the surrender of political independence, the establishment of boundaries, terms of land slaes, and related matters.

tribe A society consisting of several or many separate communities united by kinship, culture, and language, and such other social institutions as clans, religious and economic organizations, and warrior societies.

trust The legal term for the relationship between the federal government and many Indian tribes, dating from the late 19th century. Government agents managed the Indians' business dealings, including land transactions and rights to national resources, because the Indians were considered legally incompetent to manage their own affairs.

wampum Spiritually significant strings of shell beads woven to form a strip, or "belt." Used by tribes in the northeastern United States as symbols of high office and records of diplomatic negotiations, treaties and other important events. From the Algonquian word *wampumpeag*, meaning "white strings."

wigwam A one-room dome-shaped dwelling constructed of a framework of saplings or branches covered with mats or birch bark.

Xingwikaon The structure in which the displaced Delaware Indians held ceremonies that reaffirmed their culture and traditions. Also called the Big House, the building was constructed of only the natural materials that the Indians had used before their exposure to European cultures.

INDEX

PICTURE CREDITS

AP/Wide World Photos, page 94; Courtesy of William Sauts Netamuxwe Bock, pages 12, 48, 62, 73; The Brooklyn Historical Society, page 46; Culver Pictures, page 52; The Thomas Gilcrease Institute of American History and Art, Tulsa, Oklahoma, page 80; Courtesy of the Historical Society of Delaware, page 36; Courtesy of Dr. James H. Howard, pages 77, 84, 86, 102; Courtesy John T. Kraft, Seton Hall University, pages 15, 16, 17, 18, 22, 23, 30, 35, 45; Library of Congress, pages 42, 55, 58, 59, 60, 79, 82, 92, 97; Museum of the American Indian/Heye Foundation, New York, cover, pages 20, 24, 34, 65–72, 101; National Museum of American Art, Smithsonian Institution, Gift of Mrs. Harriet Harrison, page 74; National Museum of American Art, Smithsonian Institution, Gift of Mrs. Harriet Harrison, page 91; National Museum of Canada, Canadian Museum of Civilization, page 43 (neg.# S80–481B); Nelson-Atkins Museum of Art, Kansas City, Missouri (Gift of Mr. and Mrs. Lee R. Lyon), page 25; New York Botanical Garden, page 90; New-York Historical Society, New York City, page 32; New York Public Library, Astor, Lenox and Tilden Foundations, Rare Books and Manuscripts Division, pages 28, 38, 51; Courtesy of the Pennsylvania Academy of Fine Arts, Philadelphia, Gift of Mrs. Sarah Harrison, (the Joseph Harrison, Jr. Collection), page 40; Courtesy of James Rementer, page 98; The Rijksmuseum, the Netherlands Maritime Museum, page 31.

Maps (pages 2, 33, 77, 88) by Gary Tong.

ACKNOWLEDGMENTS

First and foremost, I must acknowledge my debt to my late mentor, Eleanor Burke Leacock (1922–87). The earlier drafts of this manuscript were read by several colleagues and friends, including Mark Dornstreich, Verena Hofstetter, Herbert Kraft, James G.E. Smith, and Kate Stevenson. Many Delaware people were also kind enough to comment on earlier drafts. Among them were Richard Snake, Chief of the Moravian Thames Band of Delaware Indians; Linda Poolaw, Assistant Chief of the Delaware Tribe of Western Oklahoma; Sheila Moede, of the Stockbridge-Munsee Tribe of Mohegan Indians; Jim Rementer, of the Delaware Tribe of Eastern Oklahoma; and James Lone Bear Revey, Director of the New Jersey Indian Office.

Robert S. Grumet
New Hope, Pennsylvania
Spring 1989

ROBERT S. GRUMET is Preservation Planning Branch Archaeologist with the Mid-Atlantic Region Office of the National Park Service in Philadelphia, Pennsylvania. He holds a B.A. in anthropology from the City College of New York and a Ph.D. in anthropology from Rutgers University. Dr. Grumet is the author of many articles and several books on American Indians, including *Native American Place Names in New York City* (1981) and *Native Americans of the Northwest Coast: A Critical Bibliography* (1979). He has received several grants for his research from the National Endowment for the Humanities, the National Science Foundation, the American Philosophical Society, and the D'Arcy McNickle Center for the History of the American Indian at the Newberry Library.

FRANK W. PORTER III, general editor of INDIANS OF NORTH AMERICA, is director of the Chelsea House Foundation for American Indian Studies. He holds a B.A., M.A., and Ph.D. from the University of Maryland. He has done extensive research concerning the Indians of Maryland and Delaware and is the author of numerous articles on their history, archaeology, geography, and ethnography. He was formerly director of the Maryland Commission on Indian Affairs and American Indian Research and Resource Institute, Gettysburg, Pennsylvania, and he has received grants from the Delaware Humanities Forum, the Maryland Committee for the Humanities, the Ford Foundation, and the National Endowment for the Humanities, among others. Dr. Porter is the author of *The Bureau of Indian Affairs* in the Chelsea House KNOW YOUR GOVERNMENT series.